VISITORS' HIST

NORWICH AND NORFOLK

STONE AGE TO THE GREAT WAR

VISITORS' HISTORIC BRITAIN

NORWICH AND NORFOLK

STONE AGE TO THE GREAT WAR

STEPHEN BROWNING AND
DANIEL TINK

PEN & SWORD
HISTORY

AN IMPRINT OF PEN & SWORD BOOKS LTD.
YORKSHIRE – PHILADELPHIA

First published in Great Britain in 2020 by
Pen & Sword History
An imprint of
Pen & Sword Books Ltd
Yorkshire – Philadelphia

ISBN 978 1 52670 8 427

A CIP catalogue record for this book is
available from the British Library.

Printed and bound in England by TJ International Ltd, Padstow, Cornwall

Pen & Sword Books Limited incorporates the imprints of Atlas, Archaeology,
Aviation, Discovery, Family History, Fiction, History, Maritime, Military,
Military Classics, Politics, Select, Transport, True Crime, Air World,
Frontline Publishing, Leo Cooper, Remember When, Seaforth Publishing,
The Praetorian Press, Wharncliffe Local History, Wharncliffe Transport,
Wharncliffe True Crime and White Owl.

For a complete list of Pen & Sword titles please contact

Pen & Sword Books Limited
47 Church Street, Barnsley, South Yorkshire, S70 2AS, England
E-mail: enquiries@pen-and-sword.co.uk
Website: www.pen-and-sword.co.uk

Or

Pen & Sword Books
1950 Lawrence Rd, Havertown, PA 19083, USA
E-mail: Uspen-and-sword@casematepublishers.com
Website: www.penandswordbooks.com

Dedications

This book is dedicated to my brother, Nigel John Browning.
Stephen Browning

This book is dedicated to my son, Charlie Daniel Tink.
Daniel Tink

Contents

Acknowledgements

Thanks go to the staff of all Norfolk libraries, in particular the Millennium Library in Norwich, and the British Library in London for unfailing and courteous help. There are some fine collections of materials in Norwich that are of interest to historians including local newspapers and the journals of the Norfolk and Norwich Archaeological Society. Also of help has been an online resource, the Archaeological Journal of the Royal Archaeological Institute, which has been digitally scanned and made available by the Archaeology Data Service www.archaeologydataservice.ac.uk. In addition, it is wonderful to come across all manner of individual studies that have been made by members of the Norfolk public into historical and archaeological matters, from a single coin to a complete abbey complex, that appear in many kinds of publications from those personally funded and local magazines, to the journals of prestigious societies.

Local historian David Berwick has been of immense help in researching the sections on Mundesley and Happisburgh. Thanks to author and storyteller Sarah Walker, for information on 'Diagon Alley'; at time of writing Sarah is researching a book on the underground street. We are grateful to The Missing Kind for permission to take photographs. AVIVA Archive have kindly supplied the map of fourteenth-century Norwich. Thanks to The Dean and Chapter of Norwich for allowing us to photograph the beautiful interior of Norwich Cathedral. Thanks to the Norfolk Museums Service and the National Trust for photography permission.

At Pen and Sword, we are grateful to Roni Wilkinson for all his help and advice.

Thanks to Karyn Burnham for editing and making some excellent suggestions.

Introduction

'You either get Norfolk, with its wild roughness and uncultivated oddities, or you don't. It's not all soft and lovely. It doesn't ask to be loved.'

Stephen Fry

This is the first study yet published to trace the history of Norwich and Norfolk from the time of earliest life to the outbreak of the First World War. It is divided into traveller-friendly sections for those, either singly or in groups, who wish to explore the host of fascinating places on offer in what the Norfolk-born authors believe to be the most unspoilt and mysterious county in England.

Norwich has its own section along with three possible walks taking in many of the recommended sites; for those who wish to find particular special features, each of these is highlighted in bold print in the text or can be located via the comprehensive index. The vast coast is presented next, starting at King's Lynn, which has its own walk, and proceeding in a clockwise direction around to Great Yarmouth – there is another walk here which takes in the town centre, Quays area and seafront – ending at Hopton-on-Sea. Then the book travels to central Norfolk, which is divided into west and east – the legendary Broads and the Peddars Way and Norfolk Coast Path are covered here, too. A final chapter considers Norwich and Norfolk through time using rare archive and archaeological material to give a taste of life in days gone by; special features look at life in the Regency and Victorian periods and at Norwich as the Great War approached. Appendix 1 contains a short fictional story set in 1814 incorporating genuine news items of the day. Appendix 2 features some of Norfolk's 'lost villages'.

All in all, there are over 120 photographs and illustrations, most taken especially for publication while some are rarely seen archive images.

Both of us were brought up in Norfolk and now live in Norwich; this is our sixth co-authored book on aspects of our home county. One thing we have learnt over the years is how good are our neighbours in the county at spinning a yarn. Everywhere you go there are stories and legends, often greatly embellished by multiple retellings. However, almost every tale has at least a grain of truth in it and we have gathered the most interesting together in separate sections headed 'Folklore'. We hope, by giving details of where and when these stories took root, our readers can enjoy investigating the exact degree of truth for themselves.

Throughout, telephone numbers, websites, and site details are given. There are endnotes and a bibliography designed to facilitate further study. All in all, it is hoped that readers will enjoy what is designed to be a 'toolkit' to unlock the secrets, history, sites and stories of this vast county. We wish everyone very happy travels in both space and time!

Stephen Browning – writer
www.stephenbrowningbooks.co.uk
www.facebook.com/stevebrowningbooks

Daniel Tink – photographer
www.scenicnorfolk.co.uk
www.danieltink.co.uk

Norfolk Map

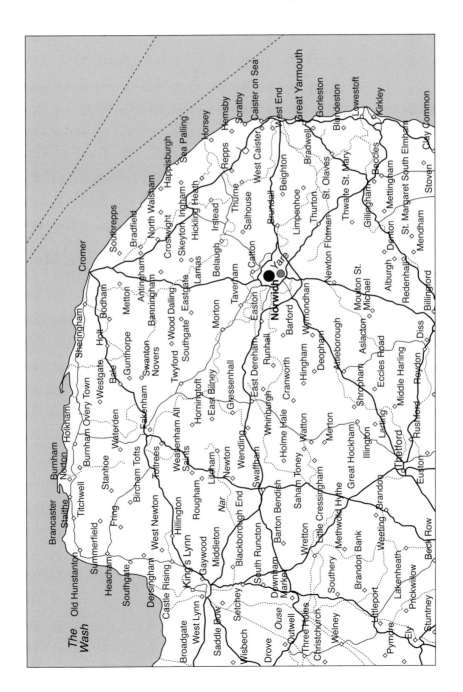

CHAPTER 1

Norwich

Norwich Cathedral

Norwich has two cathedrals, one Anglican and the other Roman Catholic. However, when people talk of 'Norwich Cathedral' they generally mean the cathedral church of the Holy and Undivided Trinity, the Anglican cathedral, situated off Tombland. It is undoubtedly Norwich's 'Jewel in the Crown' and more people probably come to visit this magnificent building than any other. You can usually see the cathedral's spire over your left or right shoulder wherever you are in the city and it is only a short walk from anywhere you may be in the central area.

Close up of Norwich Cathedral Spire

Norwich Cathedral, the cathedral church of the Holy and Undivided Trinity

From Tombland, there are two main gates. The one on your left as you stand in front of the Cathedral Close is the **Erpingham Gate**. It was built by Sir Thomas Erpingham, a knight who led the victorious English archers at the Battle of Agincourt in 1415 (details: Chapter 4). If you look up, there is a figure of him in prayer, thanking God for sparing his life during the campaign.

Ethelbert Gate, Norwich Cathedral

The other is the **Ethelbert Gate** which was built as penance by the people of Norwich following riots between monks and citizens during a fair at Tombland in 1272. Several monks were killed and they in turn locked the cathedral while employing armed men to seek retribution for their dead brothers. These men then provoked an angry mob which broke in and looted the cathedral as well as burning nearby St Ethelbert's Church. There is on record a description of the rampaging mass by a distraught monk:

> Moreover they burnt with fire the dormitory, the refectory, the guest hall, the infirmary with its chapel, and indeed all the buildings of the curia. And they slew many of the establishment, some subdeacons, some clerks, some laics in the cloister and within the walls of the monastery; others they dragged out of the walls and killed in the city or imprisoned them. And they plundered all the sacred vessels, books, gold and silver vestments, and everything that the fire had spared, for all the monks save two or three had fled from the monastery...[1]

The king was called in to mediate and sided with the monks who argued that they were governed by a higher than earthly power. The people of Norwich were told to fund the Ethelbert Gate as punishment; thirty-five were executed. It took fifty years to complete and is one of the finest examples of flint flushwork in England.

Herbert de Losinga was the man who, more than any other, is responsible for the cathedral's foundation. He committed the grave sin of simony as he paid £1,900 to have himself made Bishop of Thetford when he was 37. Appealing to the Pope for absolution, he was commanded to build a cathedral at Norwich, laying the foundation stone himself in 1096.[2]

The stone came partly from Caen in France and Barnack in Cambridgeshire. It was ferried up the River Wensum and offloaded at **Pulls Ferry**. Herbert was a strict and ambitious taskmaster and when he died in AD 1119 his successor, Eborard de Montgomery, took over. The structure was completed much as we see it today by the time he retired in AD 1145.

Many people see the **nave** as the people's church and the exquisite **choir** and **presbytery** as the monks' church as it was here that they would sing the numerous church offices starting in the early hours of the morning. The place of highest honour is behind the high altar as here are the stone remains

Pulls Ferry

of the ancient throne, the cathedra, dating probably from the eighth century. This was the seat of the bishops of East Anglia.

The cathedral has periodically during its 900 years of existence suffered great damage. In 1171 there was a major fire; in 1272, following the Tombland riots as detailed above, mobs destroyed the original Norman cloisters and killed some of the monks; the spire, at that time made of wood, was destroyed by a hurricane in 1362 and again by lightning in 1463; and vengeful Puritans looted the treasures in 1643, after which the cathedral lay in ruins for two decades.

At this time it was suggested that the stonework should be put to better use – one plan was to use it to bolster coastal defences at Great Yarmouth and elsewhere. Sometimes, damage was the result of human carelessness as this report from the *Norfolk Chronicle and Norwich Gazette*, dated 25 June 1845 makes clear:

> A fire broke out on the roof of Norwich Cathedral, and occasioned damage to the amount of £500. Bishop Manners Sutton personally distributed refreshments to

Cathedral Choir Stalls and Organ

the soldiers and others who assisted in extinguishing the flames. About 45 ft of the roof were destroyed. The fire originated from the carelessness of plumbers at work on the building.

Hitler earmarked the cathedral for maximum damage in the so-called 'Baedeker Raids' of the Second World War; remarkably, although the

Cathedral East end and apse

roof was in fact set on fire by a bomb, the bravery of two employees who clambered up and put the fire out, saved the cathedral from more extensive damage.

Even in peaceful times, the upkeep of the structure is ongoing and expensive – at least £5,000 a day. At the time of writing, although people are encouraged to buy a ticket to enter, it is not necessary if you do not wish to or cannot.

There is much to see of great beauty and some items are priceless – such as the Despenser Reredos. **The Chapel of the Royal Norfolk Regiment** is one of what used to be fourteen chapels – those on the first floor are now not accessible to the general public. The bosses on the roof tell the story of the world from the beginning of time to the Apocalypse and are pristine, being out of reach of the various marauding mobs that have damaged other parts of the church – Bishop Goldwell is, for example, without his nose on his tomb which is lacerated with sword cuts, and there is a rusted musket ball embedded in the side. Some items have a most interesting history – the Pelican Lectern, for example, was only relatively recently rediscovered buried in a garden presumably to escape the attention of looters. Legend has it that the Despenser Reredos was saved in dangerous times by hiding

Norwich Cathedral roof boss telling the story of Noah's Ark

in plain sight – it was turned over and used as the top of a workman's bench. This panel of five paintings, the finest piece of late fourteenth-century art in Europe, was given to the cathedral by Bishop Despenser in gratitude for the failure of the Peasants Revolt in 1381, which this remarkable bishop did most to savagely suppress in his other role as a military commander. Details are given below.

A feature of interest and amusement is the collection of misericords in the choir. These are small collapsible seats where it was possible for the monks to partially rest while appearing to stand during their many hours of devotions. Some of these are carved in the form of traditional biblical subjects; for example, the seven deadly sins such as gluttony, but some are humorous and it has been suggested that the craftsmen, being out of sight of their superiors, took the opportunity to have some fun. One of the most mischievous depicts a monk beating the bare buttocks of a miscreant boy. A recently carved misericord depicts a gaol being saved at Norwich Football Club.

'Mischievous Monk' Misericord

There are, of course, many monuments and plaques. One of the most notable is in the nave, a little way down from the new main entrance via the hostry if you turn right. It is called 'The Skeleton' and dates from the early 1600s. It reads:

All ye that do this place pass bye
Remember death for you must dye
As you are now even so was I
And as I am so shall ye be
Thomas Gooding here do staye
Wayting for God's Judgement Day.

Norwich Cathedral: 'The Skeleton'

There is a refectory, shop and library for use by the public; in 2009 the hostry was added. There are always spiritual, literary and musical events taking place – a highlight in summer is the production of a Shakespeare play in the cloisters; many experienced play-goers equip themselves with a cushion as sitting on a stone wall or seat for several hours can be a challenge.

Norwich citizens have their own rose – the Norwich Cathedral Rose, in pale yellow and flowering from June to November, was created for the 900th anniversary of the cathedral and launched at the Chelsea Flower Show in 1996.

Outside, the 44 acres of **The Close** offer an interesting walk with many beautiful houses of several different architectural styles. Eighty-three of these are owned by the Cathedral, many to rent if you put your name down, and are either Grade 1 or 2 listed.

Just outside the Close, heading towards the river, is Bishopsgate and here you will find **The Great Hospital.** It was begun by Bishop Walter de Suffield in 1249 and was to care for aged and infirm clergy or, in the words of the original deeds,

> principally to minister the necessaries of life to priests of the diocese of Norwich, who, broken down with age, or destitute of bodily strength, or labouring under continual disease, cannot celebrate divine service as they ought…

It also helped poor scholars, who were given free meals during term time. Thirty beds were provided for the sick poor and thirteen paupers were to be fed at the gates each day. Three masses were sung each day, including one for Bishop Suffield's soul. Today there is accommodation for 120 residents of limited means. There are tours and hospitality events.

Edith Cavell

In an area known as 'Life's Green' is the grave of Edith Cavell who was shot by the Germans in 1915 in occupied Belgium for the supposed crime of treason.

> 'Ask Father Gahan to tell my loved ones later on that my soul, as I believe, is safe, and that I am glad to die for my country'
>
> The last words of Edith Cavell

Edith Cavell was born in Swardeston, a village near Norwich, on 4 December 1865. Her father, the Reverend Frederick Cavell, something of a puritan, was vicar there for forty-five years. She was the eldest of four – her siblings being Florence, Lillian and John.

Edith grew up in the Christian faith, although reputedly finding her father's Sunday sermons boring. The rectory was far from humourless, however, as her father had the Dickensian knack of entertaining his children by dressing up, memorably as a bear, and there was much laughter in the house. Rev. Frederick was very much a man who followed up his Christian convictions, paying for much of the rectory – in which they finally settled – out of his own wages and insisting that half of Sunday lunch, following the family's trip to church, was for them and the other half for the needy of the parish.

Edith was initially educated at home but then attended Norwich High School in Theatre Street. At the age of 16 she was sent away to be educated, notably to Kensington and then Bristol, and it is at this time that she discovered the talent for foreign languages, especially French, which was to have a crucial bearing on where she went in her subsequent life.

After spending some time as a governess in Brussels, she returned to Swardeston in 1895 to nurse her sick father, and many believe that it was this experience that convinced her that she had a vocation for nursing. In 1896 she enrolled in a nurses' training course in London. Once qualified, she worked at several hospital institutions for the poor in England before being asked, in 1907, to go to Brussels where she set up and ran a course for nurses at the famed Berkendael Institute. 'Her' nurses become well-known and much sought after. It is here that we find her upon the outbreak of the Great War.

While supervising the nurses here she was asked to hide two Allied soldiers in the institute prior to their escape back to England, a request to which she agreed, successfully keeping their existence secret for two weeks. What happened next is still open to debate. Some claim that she was approached by the English Secret Services, while others claim that her actions were simply the result of compassion. At any event, she subsequently hid and helped 200 soldiers to return home.

Disaster struck on 31 July 1915 when two members of her 'escape team' were captured by the Germans. Five days later, Edith was arrested and underwent several days of intensive interrogation. This period, too, is still shrouded in mystery, as some claim that her subsequent 'confession' was the result of a trick because she was told her friends would receive a degree of leniency if she wrote down all she knew. It is possible that the Germans actually had no hard evidence up to that time, and that by filling in details of her actions in a mistaken attempt to help her friends, she actually signed her own life away.

There are two sides to War … the glory and the misery.

Edith Cavell 1915

She was kept in solitary confinement before being tried. The main language of the court was, of course, German, a language Edith did not understand. Her request to choose someone to represent her was denied and the representative for her defence was appointed by the enemy. She was convicted of treason, which many thought laughable in itself; a much more credible charge would have been espionage, which carried considerably lighter penalties. She was sentenced to be shot, a pronouncement that horrified neutral powers, such as America, and there were many frantic efforts to negotiate with the occupying Germans, all to no avail.

On the night before her death, she famously remarked that 'Patriotism is not enough', as she would willingly have helped a soldier from any country. She was shot at dawn on 12 October 1915 and hurriedly buried near to the prison by local Belgian women. Her last words are given above.

A very significant day for Norwich was when Queen Alexandra, accompanied by Princess Victoria, came to the city on 12 October 1918. She opened the Cavell Memorial Home and unveiled a memorial, the same one which can be seen today, although at the time it was situated in what would be the middle of the small roundabout at the front of the Maids Head Hotel. It was subsequently moved a few yards to its current position.

After the war moves were made to bring Edith Cavell back from Brussels to England. Her family were offered the option of burying her in Westminster Abbey in London but this was turned down in favour of the Fine City.

Exhumed on 17 March 1919, her body was found to be well preserved and the features still recognisable. On 13 May it was taken to the station, escorted by British troops on the initiative of a certain Major B.L. Montgomery (later Viscount Montgomery of Alamein), then to Ostend and from there was taken by HMS *Rowena* to Dover, where a peal of grandsire triples was rung, with all bells muffled bar the tenor. With 5,040 changes, it took three hours and three minutes. A special railway carriage bore the coffin to London on 15 May, accompanied by members of the Cavell family, and a horse-drawn gun carriage took it through streets lined with spectators to Westminster Abbey, where a funeral service was attended by George V.

Thence it travelled to Liverpool Street Station and on by train to Norwich, where the coffin was placed on another gun carriage and escorted to the cathedral by soldiers of the Norfolk Regiment for burial outside the south transept, after a service with a sermon by the Bishop of Norfolk.

The railway carriage in which her body travelled also bore that of another English hero, Captain Charles Fryatt. He was shot by the Germans after incredible heroics at sea (details: *Norfolk Coast in the Great War,* Pen and Sword 2017 by the writer) being found guilty of attempting to ram a U-boat. He was buried in Dovercourt and a steam drifter, *The Captain Fryatt,* was built in his honour at Great Yarmouth.

There is a memorial to Edith Cavell near Trafalgar Square in London; designed by Sir George Frampton, it was unveiled in 1920. There is also a Cavell Street in the East End. She is credited with making Edith a popular name for girls and, indeed, it was very common for a while, one of the most famous perhaps being Edith Piaf.

There is a memorial to her just outside the Erpingham Gate which leads into the Anglican cathedral (the gate is named after another Norwich hero, Sir Thomas Erpingham: see above) and, almost opposite, a pub bearing her name.

During the Great War itself, she is credited with encouraging tens of thousands of men to sign up. The press was incandescent in its rage and posters appeared asking who would avenge the brutal murder of this English sister of mercy by the barbarous Hun? Many enquiries about her life were directed to Swardeston including one, reported by the *Eastern Daily Press*, from an overseas admirer requesting the exact specifications of the rectory in which she was raised in order to build a replica in tribute.

She is very much still a figure of discussion today, partly because a legend has grown up around her. As already mentioned there are question marks

Edith Cavell Memorial

as to exactly how and why she did what she did. In addition, some ask why, when caught, did she attend court in day clothes, not in nursing uniform – which may have elicited sympathy – and why did she tell the truth so readily, making no attempt to be what we call today 'economical' with it? Why was she not more careful?

Edith Cavell Grave at Life's Green, Norwich Cathedral

Edith Cavell's grave is today alongside Norwich Cathedral: 'To The Pure and Holy Memory of Edith Cavell Who Gave Her Life for England'.

In recent years Peregrine falcons have been given a home on the spire of the cathedral in the hope that they will reproduce. A dedicated team of volunteers keep watch with binoculars outside. There is a website with a live cam: https://hawkandowltrust.org/web-cam-live/norwich-cathedral-side

Notes and contact details:

The cathedral is open daily from 7.30 am to 6.00 pm.

The Chapter Office is open weekdays 9.00 am to 1.00 pm and 2.00 pm to 5.00 pm. It is situated at 65, The Close, Norwich NR1 4DH. Tel: 01603 218300 email: reception@cathedral.org.uk

At the time of writing entrance is free but people are asked to consider making a payment if they are able.

Walk 1: A walk around the centre of the city

Distance: About two miles, dependent on how much you understandably wander off course here and there – there is so much of interest all around.

Time to allow: at least half a day but can quite easily take several days if you wish to linger and study interesting aspects of the city in more depth – there are also wonderful picnic spots in Chapelfield Gardens and the Plantation Gardens.

Walking conditions: If you want to go to the Roman Catholic Cathedral and Plantation Gardens, there is a fairly narrow walking bridge to negotiate which is quite steep as you go up and down – a taxi from the black cab rank on Guildhall Hill would be the best option if this is a problem. On the whole, though, apart from the slope upwards to begin with, progress is mostly on flat surfaces and is easy to navigate for wheelchairs. Take a camera!

This walk begins at the end of Exchange Street by **Jarrold Department Store** and takes in the most central part of the Fine City. Jarrold is a famous family firm originally founded in Suffolk in 1770 before moving to Norwich in 1823. The building you see now is one of the renowned designs of George

Skipper – he is also responsible for the Royal Arcade and the headquarters of Aviva in Surrey Street – and was built between 1903 and 1905. Look up to see Skipper's scenes of building and architectural work executed in local 'Cossey Ware' terracotta on the side of the store.

The route slopes upwards as you cross the road into Guildhall Hill. Ahead on the left is the **Guildhall**, beautifully finished in squared and diamond-shaped knapped flint and built at the beginning of the fifteenth century. Many people are surprised to learn that the ancient-looking clock is, in fact, a Victorian addition. For over 500 years the Guildhall served as the seat of government as well as a prison – Thomas Bilney, well-known Norwich martyr, was held in the underground cells here on the night before his burning at the stake in 1531.

Thomas Bilney was born in Norfolk in 1495 and experienced a revelation when reading the Bible, in particular a passage about Christ saving sinners, and he said that this, 'through God's instruction and inward working, which I did not then perceive, did so exhilarate my heart, being before wounded with the guilt of my sins, and being almost in despair, that immediately I felt a marvellous comfort and quietness'. He went on to become a radical preacher and fell foul of several high officials including Cardinal Wolsey. We should probably term his preaching today as basic Roman Catholicism, but he was several times pulled from the pulpit by irate listeners and in 1531 he set off for Norwich – 'my Jerusalem' – and preached in the open air. He was arrested and sentenced to death by burning at Lollards Pit (more details of the site in Walk 3, this chapter). According to Foxe's Book of Martyrs,[3] he said his private prayers before 'the officers put reeds and wood around him and lit the fire, which flared up rapidly, deforming Bilney's face as he held up his hands.' He cried 'I believe' as he died.

At the top of the hill, turn left into St Peters Street. Dominating the skyline on your right is the 'new' **City Hall**, designed by Charles Holloway James and Stephen Rowland Pierce following a competition which attracted 140 entries and was opened in 1938 by King George VI. It has never been finished as you can see if you nip around the back. The sleek Scandinavian lines do not please everybody – some slightingly call it 'the marmalade factory' on account of the colour of the bricks, and it has even been said that it is the only building in Norwich that is improved by thick fog. In the Second World

The City Hall, Guildhall and Marketplace

War Lord Haw-Haw did not like it either and announced his intention to see it flattened by German bombers. The authors' opinion is that it is a fine art deco structure that provides a happy contrast to the previous medieval Guildhall that lies below it.

The striking art deco lions flanking the front steps were seen by the architects at an exhibition in Paris and reproductions ordered. They are designed by Alfred Hardiman.

You are now standing at the 'top' of Norwich's legendary **Marketplace**. There has been a market of sorts here since William the Conqueror. Records show that it was the centre for the sale of meat, fish and fruit, later becoming important for shoe mending, silks, linen, leather and cheap bread, sometimes of dubious quality. Nowadays it is seen by the locals as somewhere to eat and browse and is a place to try a fledgling business – recent new stalls have included ones for Polish food, fine coffee and designer cakes.

In days gone by the market has also been the centre for maintaining 'discipline' in the locals. Following Kett's Rebellion in 1549, forty-five of his lieutenants were hanged, drawn and quartered here. If you were a man caught in rowdy or drunken behaviour, you would like as not spend an uncomfortable few hours in the marketplace stocks or take a flogging at the whipping post (women would be punished for similar misdemeanours by ducking stool at Fye Bridge, just off Tombland).

Once Norwich had a **Market Cross**, the outline of which can be seen today as a large red octagon cut into the ground between rows D and F of the market. It has been known for centuries that a cross existed, but it was only during renovations of the area in 2005 that its exact location was discovered.

In 1341 King Edward II had granted the city the right to hold a market in perpetuity – a right that still exists today. It was usual to erect a 'cross' to mark this privilege and, following the erection of a much smaller wooden structure, the Mayor in 1502, John Rightwise, built an imposing stone edifice which probably reached 70 ft in height at the peak. It is clear from contemporary drawings that it was a building with a cross on the top. We know from city records that in the 1570s all unemployed men of the city were required to come here at dawn in the hope of finding work for the day. A doctor was on hand to fix bones and other ailments, so illness was no excuse for non-attendance. Later it became the place where the man in charge of keeping the market clean kept his tools. Sadly, by the early eighteenth century the city's finances were in a bad way and the cross was deemed too expensive to upkeep and so it was pulled down and the stone sold for the very considerable sum of £125.

The marketplace has been the site of all manner of Norfolk life apart from the actual business of buying and selling goods, as will be seen in various parts of this study, including floggings, executions and celebrations. An example of the last, and one which did not go entirely to plan, is given in the *Norfolk Chronicle* and *Norwich Gazette* of 10 Feb 1840:

The marriage of her Majesty the Queen was celebrated in Norwich. The Mayor and members of the Corporation, wearing white favours, attended service at the cathedral, where the sermon was preached by the Rev Prebendary Wodehouse...At one o'clock the 9th Lancers, under the command of Capt Arthur Williams, entered the Market Place and fired feu de joie with their pistols; the trumpeters played 'God save the Queen', and the soldiers gave three hearty cheers, flourishing their sabres in the air....At night there was a firework display in the Marketplace. On the staging at the north-east angle of the Market Place the fireworks were prematurely exploded; a rocket was driven through the shutters of a shop on the Walk, and another entered the second storey window of a house in London Street. A man was severely wounded in the face, and others were also injured...

At the end of St Peters Street stands the ultimate in ancient and modern – **St Peter Mancroft** on your left and the **Forum**, incorporating one of the most used libraries in modern Britain, on the right. Visitors have been known to mistake 'the loveliest parish church in England' according to John Wesley, for the cathedral. The church, the largest in the city after the two cathedrals,

St Peter Mancroft – the name may derive from 'Magna Crofta' which means 'Great Meadow', upon which the church was built

was built between 1430 and 1455. It has a ring of fourteen Whitechapel bells in the western tower. Surrounding it is a fancy ironwork fence, a rare example of the work of Boulton and Paul who operated in the nineteenth century from their works near, and then on, Riverside. The firm became famous for producing almost anything in metal and invented a machine for making wire netting, greatly in demand in the colonies for controlling rabbits, and even a complete metal lighthouse in Brazil. During the First World War, production was redirected to Sopwith Camel aircraft, more of which were produced in Norwich than anywhere else.

There are many windows and monuments of interest in the church. One, the **Toppes Window** above the high altar, pictures Robert Toppes and his two wives, Alice Pert and Joan Knyvett. Robert Toppes (1400–1467) was a hugely successful entrepreneur exporting Norfolk worsted cloth and importing various goods including wine and textiles. He became City Treasurer at the age of 27, Sheriff three years later and Mayor four times. He is best known as the builder, from 1430, of **Dragon Hall** in King Street, which since 2015 has been the home of the Writers' Centre, Norwich. He is listed in the 1451 tax assessment as the richest man in Norwich, apart from the aristocracy and, on his death, he left bequests to many people, including lepers and prisoners, as well as to every church in Norwich.

A fascinating aspect of Toppes' life, and one which helps us understand the insecurity of those in power during this period, was his banishment to Bristol for four years by the king for his part in 'Gladman's Insurrection' of 1443. It is not completely clear what happened but we do know that John Gladman, a Norwich merchant and member of the Guild of St George, rode through Norwich dressed as a king with crown and sceptre, accompanied by an armed escort. In retrospect, it seems highly unlikely that an admittedly successful but relatively unknown man on the national stage could have seriously been planning to dethrone the monarch, and it is probable the procession was an unwise Shrovetide celebration. A fifteenth-century report claims that the 'revolt' was taken up by the mayor of Thetford and 3,000 others who rushed to the streets shouting 'Let us burn the Priory, kill the prior and monks'. This was enough to alarm the king, and the Mayor of Norwich, William Hempsted, was summoned to London, fined £50 and incarcerated in Fleet Prison. Legal proceedings were instigated against others in the city including Toppes, eventually being settled upon payment by Norwich of 1,000 marks. It is sometimes referred to as 'the insurrection in which no one was killed'.

A memorial with a tale to tell is situated on the wall half way down the aisle on the left as you walk towards the altar. It is made of brass and reads in part:

In Memory of Sir James Edward Smith MD FRS etc
Eldest son of James and Frances Smith of Norwich
Founder and for 40 years President of the Linnaean Society
Born at Norwich 2 December 1759 and died 17 March 1828

The society that Sir James Smith founded promoted the life and botanical work of Carl Linnaeus (1707–1778), who invented a method of classifying plants which he boasted was so straightforward that 'even women can understand it'. Earlier botanists had tried to group plants by characteristics such as the colour of their flowers or the shape of their leaves, but Linnaeus classified plants according to their reproductive organs. He used terms such as 'stamens', 'pistils', the 'bridal chamber' and 'nuptials'. For many in Britain this was seen as pornographic and there were letters in the press urging the protection of young women from the corrupting influence of botanical education and even from mixed flower-gathering expeditions. His system was retained and refined in subsequent years and he is today seen as the father of taxonomy.

Carl Linnaeus' son was named Carolus and when he died Sir James Smith bought the complete collection of his father's manuscripts for the bargain price of £1,000. In 1786 he took the works on a grand tour of Europe and founded the Linnaean Society in London upon his return in 1788. He then brought them to Norwich where he lived from 1796, publishing several thousand articles on botanical matters and becoming world-famous in the process. When he died the Linnaean Society bought all his manuscripts and those of Carl Linnaeus. The Society exists today in Piccadilly, London, and has Queen Elizabeth II as Patron while other members include the Emperor of Japan and the King of Sweden. It awards a number of prestigious medals and prizes.

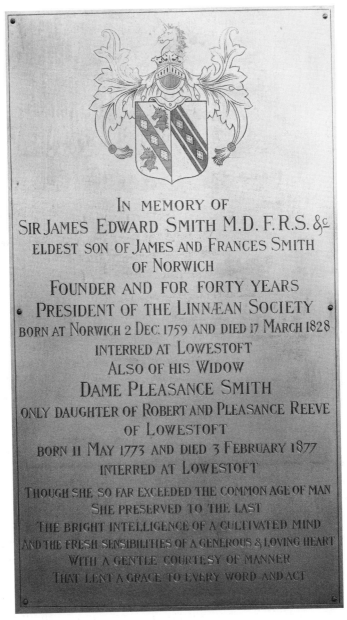

IN MEMORY OF
SIR JAMES EDWARD SMITH M.D. F.R.S. &c
ELDEST SON OF JAMES AND FRANCES SMITH
OF NORWICH
FOUNDER AND FOR FORTY YEARS
PRESIDENT OF THE LINNÆAN SOCIETY
BORN AT NORWICH 2 DEC: 1759 AND DIED 17 MARCH 1828
INTERRED AT LOWESTOFT
ALSO OF HIS WIDOW
DAME PLEASANCE SMITH
ONLY DAUGHTER OF ROBERT AND PLEASANCE REEVE
OF LOWESTOFT
BORN 11 MAY 1773 AND DIED 3 FEBRUARY 1877
INTERRED AT LOWESTOFT
THOUGH SHE SO FAR EXCEEDED THE COMMON AGE OF MAN
SHE PRESERVED TO THE LAST
THE BRIGHT INTELLIGENCE OF A CULTIVATED MIND
AND THE FRESH SENSIBILITIES OF A GENEROUS & LOVING HEART
WITH A GENTLE COURTESY OF MANNER
THAT LENT A GRACE TO EVERY WORD AND ACT

Sir James Edward Smith Memorial in St Peter Mancroft (photograph by Stephen Browning)

The Millennium Library (also known as the Forum)

The **Millennium Library**, facing St Peter Mancroft across a stepped area used by local people in summer as a good place to sit and eat food from the market below, is the Fine City's latest incarnation of a book-lending service. Norwich was the first provincial city to lend printed matter to local people in the seventeenth century, albeit only the 'higher' classes and for a fee. Offering books and education to the 'lower' classes was held by many as unsettling and unkind, as such people were surely destined to 'work and not to think'. The French Revolution in 1789 was seen as validating this argument. In addition to the city library, Tuck's famous coffee shop with a library for use by the customers set up in business from 1780 in Gentleman's Walk at the bottom of the market. Mr Tuck is also, incidentally, held to be responsible for the establishment of 'tuck shops' in public and grammar schools throughout Britain and the Empire, dreaming of which get schoolchildren through double Maths right up to this day.

Turn right by the library and walk up Bethel Street. Approaching Little Bethel Street on your left you will see a plaque high on the wall. This commemorates Mary Chapman as this is the site of her revolutionary asylum for 'curable lunaticks', which she opened in the early eighteenth century.

It was remarkable in its time for being free, and the 1728 records show that it housed twenty-eight patients. It lasted well into the twentieth century before being converted into flats and offices.

At the end of Little Bethel Street, cross the busy road into **Chapelfield Gardens**. This was where locals in Victorian times would gather around the still-existing bandstand and listen to a selection of religious and uplifting music. Previously it was also the venue for compulsory archery practice for men in the thirteenth and fourteenth centuries and is reputed to have been the training ground for the archers under Sir Thomas Erpingham who won the battle of Agincourt in 1415. Sir Thomas himself is commemorated by the Erpingham Gate, one of the two main entrances to the Anglican Cathedral in Tombland. When visiting the area, look up to see a carving of him in prayer, thanking God for having saved his life. Chapelfield Gardens was also the venue of troop practice in the Great War and sometimes chaotic manoeuvres by the Home Guard at the beginning of the Second World War.

The first signs of Spring as thousands of crocuses appear in Chapelfield Gardens

Folklore

The ghost that liked Beethoven's Fifth

This is a story, never before printed, and told to the authors by a friend. To protect privacy, his name and that of the central-Norwich church are omitted. He is well known in the city and not of a fanciful nature:

I was asked to play the organ at a planned wedding in the church and went along to try it out on a cold, wet November evening at about 8 ish. I am not at all spooked by empty churches and was looking forward to learning about the organ. Oh! It was marvellous, rich and booming with a wonderful clear tone. I played a little gentle Mozart and then thought I would try the opening chords to Beethoven's Fifth as they are so dramatic. Suddenly, I became conscious of another person in the church and looked up in the mirror which is designed so that the organist can keep his eyes on what is going on in the nave behind him. There, silently passing by, was the figure of a woman dressed in a fitted bodice and long skirt – she was not walking, more floating and I noticed that the lower part of her legs appeared to be below floor level, so I could only see her from half way up her calf. I would not say she was a white figure, more of a parchment colour and very musty. She did not seem interested in me at all. That is all I saw as I am not afraid to say I was terrified and rushed out of the church and headed for home. Well, that's not quite the end of it as I pondered during the next few days on what I had seen; I didn't tell anyone, even my wife, in case they laughed but I thought I just had to go back and check it out or I would never get over it! So I went back again at about the same time, set up and checked there was no one there. Then – da da da dah! – the beginning of Beethoven's Fifth. Guess what? She was there again. This time I turned round on my organist's seat and watched her as she floated up the aisle and vanished through the altar and end wall. I did not feel afraid at all this time. Anyway, an interesting thing is that I did a bit of research and found that the floor level had been raised in the eighteenth century which may explain why I couldn't see her feet. I have no explanation why she was 'floating' though or who she was.[4]

If you walk up to the end of Chapelfield Gardens farthest from the city you can see looming ahead of you, across some very busy roads and a roundabout, the **cathedral church of St John the Baptist**. The only safe way to cross the roads is by a footbridge spanning the busy dual carriageway of Grapes Hill and you can reach this by exiting the gardens by the last exit, far right. You will find yourself on Earlham Road and the entrance to the cathedral is on your left.

The man credited with the vision to create this fine building is Henry, 15th Duke of Norfolk (1847–1917) who wanted to restore the Roman Catholic faith to pre-eminence. He had married Lady Flora Hastings in 1877 and the church was to be a 'thank-you' to God for his happiness.

Originally a church of extraordinary proportions, and only created a cathedral by the Pope in 1976, it is built on the former site of Norwich gaol. It is designed by George Gilbert Scott Jr, and there were many problems during construction because of chalk caves underneath the surface. The area is noted for potholes and sinkholes, one famous example of which opened

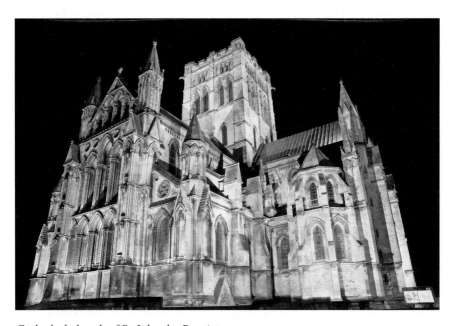

Cathedral church of St John the Baptist

up and partially 'swallowed' a double decker bus on the road outside in the 1950s. Also the stone used – Devon Beer as opposed to Caen and Carnac stone for the Anglican cathedral – was found to be too soft for purpose and today parts of the exterior are quite worn down. Certainly, the cathedral church of the Holy and Undivided Trinity appears generally in far better condition despite being 800 years older. The duke himself was to lose his wife at the age of 34 and his son and heir was born blind. However, despite all these problems he persevered and the church was opened in 1910. **The Narthex**, with café, bar, meeting, business and function rooms was opened exactly 100 years later. The **Duckett Library** holds about 4,000 religious publications.

Inside the overall impression is of French Gothic splendour – dark, rich and detailed. Everywhere there are pillars of many sizes made of brown Durham marble in each of which can be seen thousands of fossilised creatures. Looking down from the west, the chancel is a little off-centre and this is because it represents Christ on the cross with his head to one side. Henry the 15th Duke designed the window representing the Queen of Heaven and the Christ Child in the north transept and Gwendolen, his second wife, donated the Walsingham chapel.

Literally a few yards along the road is the site of the **Plantation Gardens**, often referred to as the 'secret garden', partly because many locals are unaware of its existence and partly because it does have a magical quality. A gentle slope down leads to the entrance where there is an honesty box asking for £2 per person.

Sometimes called 'a rich man's folly', it was built by Henry Trevor, a wealthy Norwich cabinet maker, between 1856 and 1896. Its 3 acres have pathways up, down and round about, passing fancy brickwork, fountain, instant 'ruins' and beautiful lawns and flower beds. It used to have a Palm House in the glory days. It is a unique place to have a picnic.

Neglected for forty years after the Second World War it has been restored and is now run by a trust consisting of volunteers. You can join the trust for a fee and come along to special ticketed events such as an Annual Summer Fete.

The garden was closed for a while and tests carried out in 2016 and 2017 as old mining tunnels and sinkholes caused collapses inside or nearby. At the time of writing, all is well and the garden fully open.

The Nave of the cathedral church of St John the Baptist (photograph by Stephen Browning)

Retrace your steps now to head back to town. Cross over the footbridge again and, at the end of St Giles Street, bear right and walk down Theatre Street, passing, on your right, the **Theatre Royal** which is very impressive following a multi-million pound restoration. The theatre attracts top names to its productions and has been called 'London's West End in Norwich'.

Pass the **Assembly House**, also famed in days gone by for theatrical productions, and, opposite **St Stephen's Church** – newly underpinned after water compromised the foundations – take William Booth Street into Hay Hill. Here you will see a statue to Sir Thomas Browne. Sir Thomas was a writer on medical matters and a local magistrate. He was an early pioneer of what we today call 'alternative medicine', and created a celebrated herb garden which is now a car park in the Cathedral Close. One of his most famous written works was an essay *Hydriotaphia, Urn-Burial* of 1658, which is a study of fifty funeral urns in Norfolk and this in turn prompts reflections on life, death, and immortality. He also recorded the discovery of Iceni coins. He was knighted by Charles II when he visited the city in 1671.

A contemporary account of his character has this to say:

He was a person of most extensive learning and profound judgement; very eminent in his medical profession, and of extensive practice: he was a sincere professor of the religion of the church of England, which he dignified with his unaffected piety, strict morality, unbounded charity, and benevolence: his probity rendered him universally respected, and his benevolence generally beloved: in his person he was comely and venerable, as appears from his picture, which hangs in the vestry of St Peter Mancroft Church.

Note: the picture is still there.

Among many famous quotes by Sir Thomas is: 'Be able to be alone. Lose not the advantage of solitude, and the society of thyself.'

Of himself, he said: 'I am the happiest man alive. I have that in me that can convert poverty to riches, adversity to prosperity, and I am more invulnerable than Achilles; Fortune hath not one place to hit me.' He did suffer misfortune after his death in that his coffin was accidentally broken by a workman in 1840 and his skull taken. It came into the possession of

Norfolk and Norwich Hospital in 1847 by means unknown, and after an argument during which the hospital refused to give it up, claiming that there was no means of conferring ownership, the vicar of St Peter Mancroft made an official request to regain the skull in 1893. The hospital, possibly embarrassed about how it came into their possession, said that there were no records of its acquisition but that such a request was quite unprecedented. Rumours grew that it was a fake, but after an examination proved it to be that of Sir Thomas Browne, it was given back and re-interred in its rightful place in 1921. Five casts were made, one of which remained at the hospital, one was given to St Peter Mancroft, one is in Norwich Museum, one in the Royal Society of Medicine and the other is currently in the Royal College of Surgeons in London.

Walking downhill brings you to the **Haymarket** which, in turn leads on **Gentleman's Walk**. Here, in the seventeenth and eighteenth centuries, gentlemen would parade up and down in their finery, dropping now and again into a coffee house such as 'Tuck's', already mentioned, to discuss the state of the world and to read newspapers. Parading in your own way up this elegant concourse will bring you, on your right, to **George Skipper's Royal Arcade**. This is a magnificent riot of peacocks, art-deco tiles and extravagant lighting. This was, for many years, the site of a shop selling goods made by Colmans.

Mustard is Norwich's most celebrated export. Jeremiah Colman established a huge business down by the river refining the yellow paste, later expanding into starch, laundry blue and other products. What is most remarkable, however, is that he set standards of care for the workforce that were unheard of in eighteenth-century England. There was a medical team, a school for the workers' children and Mrs Colman herself used to cook the employees a lunch of stew, bread and coffee for four old pennies (4d). Trips were organised for the workforce. Even a model village was created with decent housing. When he died the crowds flocking to his funeral were said to be as big as for any funeral ever seen, including in London. He is buried in Rosary Cemetery.

Walking through the Royal Arcade, up a gentle slope and then half a dozen steps brings you to Castle Meadow, where a good few buses stop, and ahead of you looms **Norwich Castle**.

The Royal Arcade

Norwich Castle

The castle, often referred to by locals as 'The Square Box on the Hill', was started by William the Conqueror in 1067 and finished in the main by 1121. The main structure, of Caen stone, stands on a flint base and would once have housed a community complete with houses, stables and workshops. Stone was very expensive and transportation trebled the cost. Between 1834 and 1839 it was resurfaced in Bath stone.

Serving as the county gaol from the fourteenth century, it became a museum from 1894 when the gaol had moved to Mousehold Heath. It now holds over 3 million objects, many of national significance and it houses a **Study Centre** for the decorative arts, archaeology and natural history. You can visit the soul-sapping dungeons where criminals were kept, sometimes before being hanged, and can inspect the plaster casts of the heads belonging to those executed. There was once a belief that the shape of the head indicated various personality traits including the propensity to criminality and violence and thus these samples were kept for study.

Various imaginative ways have been created to experience life in days gone by – one of the most popular is the Fighting Gallery Tour. A trip to the battlements may be possible subject to health and safety factors – best to check on this before travelling. Putting on a medieval 'crown' and robe before sitting on a wooden medieval 'throne' is popular!

In October 2018 it was announced that the castle had secured a £9.2 million grant from the National Lottery to redevelop the keep and make extensive restorations within, including putting back the ancient flooring. The funding is for a new gallery, also, with objects loaned by the British Museum.

Early in 2019 Norwich Museum announced that it had obtained the final pieces from the unique Binham hoard. The gold bracteates – pendants – were buried in Binham in the sixth century and it is the largest gold hoard yet found from sixth-century Britain. The bracteates are a very rare form of Scandinavian jewellery and will have belonged to people who migrated here; they point to Binham's importance as a centre at this time. Details of the Priory at Binham are given below.

When you leave the castle, turn right and skirt the circumference of the keep along Castle Meadow. Across the road there are shops, and under number 21, formerly Ponds Shoe Shop and at the time of writing a café called The KindaKafe, is what locals often refer to as the entrance to Norwich's own Diagon Alley, an underground ancient passageway. The streets behind these shops – London St and Castle St – are at a much lower level than Castle Meadow which means that the shops themselves, such as Boots or Waterstones, are split level with stairs linking the two floors. This came about as once Castle Meadow was on a lower level, too, but the filling-in of the vast ditches around the castle raised it up. Among many interesting features in the alley is the carving of the number 1739 on a wall – a date or perhaps a number of shoes? There are also the initials 'B.G.' and a St Andrew's Cross enclosed in a frame – similar graffiti to the latter can be found in the Anglican cathedral (pictured in the authors' book *Spirit of Norwich Cathedral* PiXZ). Research is ongoing into the structure – which includes flint walls, oak panels and wattle-and-daub plasterwork with horsehair – but for now, visitors can take a look on an accompanied tour.

This walk ends here, leaving you in the centre of town.

This underground ancient alley is a remnant of what a great deal of Norwich must have been like. Photos taken with kind permission from The Missing Kind

Given below are many Norfolk finds and remains. An early Victorian writer had this to say:

> The position of Norfolk on the Eastern coast of the kingdom forbids it possessing the more important Celtic remains – the Cairn, the Cromlech, the Rock Basin, the Rocking Stone, the engraved Pillar, the Circle of Stones, objects so remarkable on the Western shores. But Barrows, with their contents, Celts, Spear-heads, Beads, etc, and other vestiges of the ruder times, are found scattered throughout its whole surface.[5]

Many ancient finds have been found in and around Norwich itself as building works are undertaken, as well as by amateur detectorists. One of the most interesting sites is **Easton**, about seven miles west of the city. Neolithic to early Bronze Age flints, pottery, and evidence of cremations are here. The most spectacular find was in 1851 when 4,000 copper-alloy coins were

Oak panels laid against a flint wall, underneath a jetty that the Archaeological Society reports is Tudor

'The Dungeon': despite the caged window, no evidence exists that supports the theory of this once having actually been a dungeon. However many bailiffs were listed in trade directories as living along Castle Meadow and before 1820 they were allowed to privately imprison debtors

uncovered by perhaps the landlord of the local pub (records from this time are unfortunately not precise).

Travelling out of Norwich on the B1149 (Holt Road) for six miles brings you to the site of **Horsford Castle**. All that remains now is a fairly flat motte and bailey, but once the motte was over 80 yards square. It was built by Walter de Caen who was granted the manor of Horsford as a reward for fighting for Henry I. Walter's son, Robert, having been released from vagabonds after praying to St Faith, founded the **Monastery to St Faith** near the castle. Both sites were probably abandoned around 1450.

Flordon is a village south of Norwich and it was here in 2013 that a rare medieval seal was found.

South of Norwich, on the A140 Norwich to Ipswich Road, opposite the church, lies what is named the **Tasburgh Enclosure**. It is easy to reach by

Horsford Castle, Motte and Bailey remains

bus from Norwich centre. The much altered site was perhaps an Iron Age fort, or possibly dates from Saxon times as much pottery of this period has been found. It is now owned by the Norfolk Archaeological Trust and more excavation is needed to unlock its secrets. For the moment there are two explanation panels for visitors and it is free to see.

Further finds in Norwich are discussed in Chapter 4.

Notes and contact details:

Eating and drinking in Norwich city centre. There are two food courts in Castle and Chapelfield Shopping Malls. Most national chains operate in Norwich and all can be found within the compact central area. Two supermarkets offer the usual selection of sandwiches, take-away snacks and drinks. In addition, there is the marketplace which has a number of take-away outlets, offering Italian, Chinese, Polish, Mexican, Turkish, traditional British, Vegetarian and Vegan foods – there are seats bordering the market and many people use the steps of the Forum to sit and eat in fine weather. Chapelfield Gardens are a few minutes away and popular as a picnic spot. Jarrold has several restaurants well-used by the locals. The top floor restaurant – there is a lift – is very busy all day beginning with excellent breakfasts using local ingredients. At lunchtimes there is a traditional carvery and extensive salad bar www.jarrold.co.uk 01603 66066. Five Guys is a new and popular venue in Orford Place for burger lovers (www.fiveguys.co.uk 01603 620763). Those who like Caribbean cuisine in a colourful and friendly setting could try Turtle Bay in Swan Lane (www.turtlebay.co.uk 01603 305380). The Waffle House in St Giles Street, specialising in Belgian waffles, both sweet and savoury, is something of a Norwich institution (www.wafflehousenorwich. co.uk 01603 612790). For the ultimate in afternoon tea – they do 'themed' teas as well which in the past have included a Halloween Frightful Fancies Tea and another based on magic – try the Assembly House in Theatre Street (www.assemblyhousenorwich.co.uk 01603 626402). In addition, there is a fair array of establishments offering specialist menus such as New York Deli, Asian, Spanish, Dutch, and Japanese food. For details visit www. visitnorwich.co.uk/eat-and-drink/

The Maids Head Hotel in Tombland, Norwich is thought to be the oldest hotel in the UK, dating back 800 years

Accommodation. The Maids Head Hotel on Tombland, which once reputedly put up Queen Elizabeth I, is the city's most famous but certainly not the most expensive www.booking.com.maidsheadhotel/norwich 01603 209955. The Assembly House, opposite the Forum and mentioned above offers beautiful rooms and suites. The budget traveller will find the best area to explore is alongside and at the back of Thorpe Station. Both Premier Inn and Travelodge operate centrally and there is a Holiday Inn next to Carrow Road Football Ground. An excellent alternative at very reasonable prices is University of East Anglia guest accommodation – open to everybody and not just the families of students. If you prefer not to use a car, buses – numbers 25 and 26 on the Blue Line – run 24/7 to and from the university and take about fifteen minutes to the city centre. Check out: https://www.uea.ac.uk/about/visiting-staying/visitor-accommodation

For help generally and other options www.visitnorwich.co.uk/stay

Pubs. Sadly, there are not as many as there used to be and the situation is constantly changing, but some still thrive. The Bell Hotel, next to the castle, and where you could once hire a room to watch a hanging, is generally packed and the Sir Garnet – opened as a pub in 1861 – on the marketplace is still there. The Glass House is a large Wetherspoon pub off Tombland, famous for its breakfasts from 8.00 am. The Adam and Eve, south of the Cathedral Close, is Norwich's oldest pub, having started life in about 1249 as a drinking establishment run by Benedictine monks for the workers building the cathedral. Along the river, just a few yards from Thorpe Station, is The Queen of Iceni, which has an extensive menu and overlooks the water. (There is also a bowling alley and multiplex cinema here – the other Norwich multiplex is a few yards from the Bell Hotel, above.)

CAMRA runs hugely successful Norwich Beer Festivals and other events often in June and October www.norwichcamra.org.uk

Norwich Tourist Information Centre, Forum, Norwich
tourism@norwich.gov.uk. Tel: 01603 213999
Open Monday to Saturday 9.30 am – 5.30 pm
Information on events, walks, guided tours, places of interest and
   sales of souvenirs and maps. Sharing the same site is Jarrolds local
   store which stocks the best in Norwich and Norfolk products such

as honey, books, art work, cards, candles and soap. It is open seven
days a week. forumshop@jarrold.co.uk 01603 727922

British playwright James Dimelow has scripted an entertaining
short-film about the Assembly House www.newplays.org.uk/
assembly-house-norwich-animation

Norwich Castle Museum and Art Gallery, Castle Hill, Norwich,
NR1 3JU https://www.museums.norfolk.gov.uk/norwich-castle
email: museums@norfolk.gov.uk. Tel: 01603 493625
Opening times: weekdays 10.00 am until 4.30 pm and Sundays
1.00 pm until 4 pm. (May change at times of building and
renovations so best to check in advance.)

For details of tours of Norwich's Diagon Alley: 01603 850309,
www.missingkind.org

Roman Catholic Cathedral of St John the Baptist, Cathedral House,
Unthank Road, Norwich NR2 2PA 01603 624615 email:
admin@sjbcathedral.org.uk

Mass is celebrated at 10.00 am Monday to Friday, at 6.00 pm on
Saturday and at 9.00 am and 11 am on Sundays. The tower is
open to visitors in summer at 1.30 pm and 2.30 pm – the views
are spectacular. There is a shop and café open during the day.
Educational trips are welcomed and teachers should email
education@stjohncathedral.co.uk

Walk 2: Around the Norwich Lanes

A walk through St Benedicts Street, Cow Hill, Upper St Giles Street, Pottergate
and the Lanes, taking in Maddermarket Theatre and Strangers' Hall.

Distance*:* 1–2 miles, dependent on how much you are tempted to wander
off course here and there.

Time to allow*:* at least two hours for a fairly brisk walk – longer if you
linger.

Walking conditions: On the whole fairly flat or gently sloping, but quite
steep going up Cow Hill (total distance of a few hundred yards). Although
there are a few steep steps elsewhere it is possible to avoid these by checking
alongside for pathways. Take a camera!

The famous Swan found in the Norwich Lanes

To start this walk you need to 'drop down' from the town centre to **St Benedicts Street**. Resisting the temptation to go down the steps and heading straight on, a slow stroll down St Benedicts Street will reveal four churches and an eclectic array of shops, pubs and cafés. Notice the **Norwich Arts Centre** on your right as you walk down the street – an imaginative use of an old church. There is live music, interactive exhibitions, storytelling, poetry nights, live music, photographic courses and all sorts of things taking place in the centre. It also contains a peaceful café.

Almost opposite the Arts Centre, turn left into Ten Bell Lane where the walk starts to get quite steep. On the corner with **Pottergate**, you will pass the Micawber Tavern, named after the famous character in Dickens' *David Copperfield* who always believed that 'something will turn up'. Walk straight ahead and up **Cow Hill** towards the imposing church of **St Giles-on-the-Hill**. At the top of the hill turn right into **Upper St Giles Street**. This is a pretty street where you can dine in some first-class restaurants – advance booking recommended. It also houses some of the city's most notable delicatessens and patisseries where everything from homemade organic scotch eggs to take-away crème brulees are available. You will pass some shops selling reclaimed architectural treasures and antiques.

The street comes to a sudden end as the Grapes Hill dual carriageway cuts rudely across it. A fine view of the **Roman Catholic Cathedral** is in front of you which makes for an amazing visit, as does the **Plantation Garden** beside it (see Walk 1 for details).

On the way home, cross the street and start to walk back along Upper Giles Street.

At the top of the road is a plaque commemorating that fine English actor Sir John Mills, who went to school here. Apparently, he hated it. Sir John provides another link to Charles Dickens in the public mind because one of his most celebrated roles was Pip in the 1946 film of *Great Expectations*.

Charles Dickens loved Norfolk. Some of his greatest writing features the county – notably Great Yarmouth which stars in *David Copperfield*, Dickens' favourite of all his novels. His attitude to it must have been a little ambivalent, however, because in a private letter to his agent in 1849, he referred to the city as 'a spongy and soppy place'. In *The Pickwick Papers*, Mr Pickwick and Sam Weller, the characters that propelled him to international fame at the age of 25, also had some memorable adventures in Norfolk. Famously, the hilarious description of an election at Eatanswill in the book is a critical but affectionate comment on Norwich. Dickens writes that '…the Eatanswill people, like the people of many other small towns, considered themselves of the utmost and most mighty importance…'. He might well have been standing in St Giles Street as he said this. It is also documented that he came here (to the castle) to witness one of the last public hangings and that he was appalled at what he saw. Thereafter, he campaigned against this barbaric practice, particularly the 'party atmosphere' of the proceedings. He was a hero in his own lifetime and is credited with helping to change the people's attitude to public punishments.[6]

Walk back down the street and past the church of **St Giles-on-the-Hill**, the gardens of which, in Spring and Summer are a riot of colour in a classic English way with giant specimens of hollyhocks and foxgloves almost hiding the lower parts of the church walls. A wonderful lilac wisteria winds around the wall beside the road. Turn sharp left down Willow Lane; just where it

The church of St Giles is especially beautiful in Spring when its walls are covered in Wisteria

meets Cow Hill on your right is a plaque commemorating George Borrow – the man who coined the term 'Norwich – A Fine City' – who lived here.

George Borrow

'A Fine City' was coined by the writer George Borrow in 1851. Actually what he wrote in *Lavengro* was, 'A Fine old city, truly is that...', but the word 'old' was later omitted.

It did not catch on straightaway. As late as the First World War many referred to Norwich as 'No Mean City', which was taken from St Paul's description of Tarsus. Even later the city council had the idea of calling Norwich 'England's Other City', which did not last. Sometimes now the press will refer to 'Norwich, England's only UNESCO City of Literature'.

George Borrow (1803–1881) went as a 'free boy' to Norwich Grammar School, a humiliation some say he never got over, as the 'free boys' were looked down on by the boarders who tended to be the sons of middling gentlefolk like clergy and solicitors.

He is famous for four books. The first, and many consider the best by far, is *The Bible in Spain*, which recounts his adventures distributing bibles in Spain, a land of incredible hardship and beauty at the time. Some critics argue that the book suffers very slightly from the hero's (i.e. George Borrow's) description of what a fine chap he is, but this was readily forgiven. Here is a taste of it:

> It was near sunset … and we were crossing the bay of Gibraltar Bay! It seemed no bay, but an inland sea, surrounded on all sides by enchanted barriers, so strange, so wonderful, was the aspects of its coasts. Before us lay an impregnable hill; on our right, the African continent, with its grey Gibil Muza and the crag of Ceuta to which a solitary bark seemed steering its way; behind us the town we had just quitted, with its mountain wall; on our left the coast of Spain … There, at the base of the mountain, and covering a small portion of its side, lay the city, with its ramparts garnished with black guns pointing significantly at its moles and harbours …

This book was immediately incredibly successful, *The Examiner* saying: 'Never was a book more legibly impressed with the unmistakable mark of genius.' George Borrow became a society sensation, attending all manner of parties until everything became too much and he ran away. He found instant fame of this magnitude almost impossible to take. But eight years later, egged on by his publisher, he produced another, probably his most famous – *Lavengro* – and followed this with *The Romany Rye*. The books are loosely autobiographical. Timewise, *Lavengro* covers several years, but *The Romany Rye* (the title means 'the Gypsy Gentleman' which refers to how the author was often unkindly seen by the sons of the gentry at Norwich Grammar School) covers only several weeks. Some critics once again said – as they had about *The Bible in Spain* – that the main function of the books was to prove how learned and talented was George Borrow. Sometimes, however, the writing is reminiscent of Charles Dickens who was at the peak of his fame at this time, having just finished serialising *Little Dorrit*. The following is an example. It is describing the start of an argument between two groups of people below Edinburgh Castle:

> It was a beautiful Sunday evening, the rays of the descending sun were reflected redly from the grey walls of the Castle, and from the black rocks on which it was founded. The bicker had long since commenced. Stones from sling and hand were flying; but the callants of the New Town were now carrying everything before them.

Unfortunately the reviews for the two new books were appalling, which caused a man of Borrow's temperament great pain. One critic said that the 'books are, in short, clogged with material that is not good enough or not good at all'. Others pointed to an almost total lack of structure.

His final known book was reluctantly published by Murray, his publisher, in 1862 – the firm was not at all convinced that it would sell after the slating given to the previous two. It was a description of a trip taken by Borrow and his wife and called *Wild Wales*. It did very well, making over £500 profit. Alas, however, reviews were not good and this was far more important to Borrow than money. One magazine called it 'extremely defective' and 'intensely prosaic'.

He spent a good part of his later life in Great Yarmouth and Norwich. He was often to be seen walking for hours on Mousehold Heath which inspired the famous saying from chapter 25 of *Lavengro:* 'There's the wind on the Heath, brother; if I could only feel that, I would gladly live for ever.' He died aged 79, taking regular exercise and swimming to the last. He is buried in Brompton Cemetery in London.

You are never very far away from George Borrow in the centre of Norwich. He is known to have stayed at a lodging house on the site of the present Forum; he attended entertainments at the Assembly House; one of his characters in *Lavengro* lived on Hay Hill; an early publisher had premises in Gentleman's Walk; he himself has a plaque on Cow Hill; and, unsurprisingly as he attended Norwich School, the Erpingham Gate is mentioned in *Lavengro*.

There is a George Borrow society – www.georgeborrow.org. Followers call themselves 'Borrovians'.

Back on the walk, turn right into **Pottergate.** This ancient street has been the centre of many trades. The name derives from the pottery industry that existed prior to the thirteenth century. Shoe manufacturing peaked in the eighteenth and nineteenth centuries. An eye infirmary established here eventually became incorporated with the Norfolk and Norwich Hospital. The famous, and widely idolised opera singer, **Jenny Lind**, established a **Hospital for Sick Children** here in mid-Victorian times. More recently, it became the home of Norwich Job Centre and some English Language Schools – a modern-day Norwich industry. George Borrow pops up all over the city and here is no exception as he lived in Pottergate for a period.

Ahead is **St Gregory's Alley.** A pleasant grass area with refurbished seating, it is an oasis for many folk who sit down, on the grass, seating or low walls in front of St Gregory's Pottergate, to have a bite. There is a delicatessen, a fish and chip shop, some sandwich bars and a juice bar all within a few yards. St Gregory's Pottergate is now a craft centre with a café and 'The Birdcage' Pub borders the green. You are now at the very centre of Norwich Lanes. As you walk around, note the refurbished street furniture and the green and gold square plaques inserted into the walkways which tell tales of life and businesses in days gone by.

There are three more important stops on this walk. One of them is **The Bridewell** in Bridewell Alley which tells the story of Norwich industry – mustard, textiles, chocolate and beer. The building itself is a sombre flint

The Museum of Norwich at the Bridewell

edifice and it is not hard to believe that it was once a prison for beggars – 'bridewells' – and women. If you go around the building to the opposite side you will find the original small oak doorway, blackened, cracked with age and extensively repaired, through which prisoners passed to begin their sentence.

Carry on a few yards until you come to St John's Alley which runs down the side of a fine small church, **St John Maddermarket**, which houses the finest collection of brasses in the city. The name 'Maddermarket' is derived from 'madder', which is a Norfolk plant that produces a red dye. Half way down, you will come across **The Maddermarket Theatre**. This is special because it welcomes local people to act and help out in putting on professional productions. There is also a plaque commemorating the feat of the most famous Morris dancer of all time, Will Kemp. In 1599, for a bet, he morris-danced ('lustily', according to his tomb in London) all the way from London to Norwich. It took him four weeks and he ended his journey, to great acclaim, in this alley where he jumped over the graveyard wall of St John Maddermarket opposite the theatre entrance. He was rewarded with a pension of forty shillings a year.

The Maddermarket Theatre

At the bottom of this alley is an ancient water pump that served the needs of the area.

Somewhere in this vicinity during the reign of Elizabeth I was the **Palace of the Duke of Norfolk,** and we know from the letters of guests that it was a malodorous place, being too close to the river into which raw sewage was pumped. It is here that he plotted to marry Mary, Queen of Scots, losing his head as a consequence.

At Charing Cross, turn left and a few more steps will find you at **Strangers Hall**. The building itself dates from 1320 and contains imaginative recreations of life in Tudor and Stuart times. In the Great Hall, the high table is set for a feast which gives an inkling of the excessive carbohydrate diet eaten by wealthy merchants prior to modern-day notions of healthy eating.[7] The seventeenth-century bedroom of Lady Paine (wife of Mayor, Sir Joseph Paine) is open to public view. There is a collection of historic toys, too. A costumed guide will show you around. It is open 10.30 am–4.30 pm Wednesday and Saturday. A charge is made for entry.

This walk ends here – you are a few yards from where it began.

Walk 3: Riverside

Distance: 3-4 miles, dependent on how much you wander off course now and again.

Time to allow: 3-4 hours, or longer if you have a drink or meal, perhaps in the pubs and restaurants on Riverside or in Magdalen Street.

Walking conditions: Easy and flat for the most part with a gentle slope up to the city centre at the end. Magdalen Street, the last section, has very narrow pavements. Take a camera!

This walk begins in **Tombland** (nothing to do with tombs, although thousands are probably buried here, but derived from the ancient Norse word for 'empty space'). Enter the **Cathedral Close** and walk down the gentle slope to **Pulls Ferry** – where stone from Caen was unloaded to build the cathedral in the twelfth century – passing the playing fields of Norwich School. Turn right and follow the river to the Compleat Angler pub where you will need to cross the road before dropping down to follow the river again. In about ten minutes you will come to the **Carrow Road**

View of Tombland from the pretty garden of the church of St George

Football Ground. Turn back and take the Wherry Road which runs parallel with the river.

The Norwich football team is known as 'The Canaries'. Once, the city was the pre-eminent breeding centre for the birds, one of the most common species of which have yellow and green plumage and this has been adopted as the team's colours. The club officially came into existence in 1902 before becoming bankrupt after the Great War as many of the team's most talented young men signed up in 'Pals' Units. A very early song on the terraces went like this:

> To our Norwich City we mean to bring fame,
> With our Norwich City we'll play such a game,
> That Fulham and Tottenham will faint at the name,
> Of Norwich Canaries, what-ho!

Another famous firm adjacent to the stadium since the 1850s was Colmans. Jeremiah Colman was a very popular employer and in many ways far ahead of his time; he built an ideal village for his workers, provided lunch and medical facilities for them as well as a school for their children. At the time of writing the future of the Norwich-based activities of Colmans, since taken over by Unilever, is uncertain. However, Norwich and Colmans will always be famous for mustard. A well-known slogan of the nineteenth century was 'Come on Colmans. Light my Fire'.

Walking back now towards the city, you will gain a wonderful view of the Anglican Cathedral ahead of you and see, on the river, the remains of a **boom tower**. These structures – Cow Tower is another later on in this walk – were designed to control the movement of boats in and out of the city. Chains would be slung across the water and the wherrys that used to trade in chimney pots, stone and other goods, would be allowed to progress after payment of a fee.

Just past the **Novi Sad Friendship Bridge** (Norwich is twinned with a town of that name in Serbia) turn left towards the water's edge and you will see two starkly beautiful modern sculptures in iron and copper which

The remains of a boom tower on the River Wensum

celebrate one of the Fine City's most important firms which operated where you stand – Boulton and Paul. The firm began in 1797 as an ironmongery shop in what is now Little London Street and in 1864 moved to Rose Lane. In 1867 it perfected a machine for the manufacture of wire netting and found that it could not keep up with the demand from the colonies, especially Australia which was having trouble controlling rabbits. By the early years of the twentieth century it had the capability of producing almost anything in metal including a complete lighthouse in Brazil. In the Great War the firm diversified into aircraft production and produced more of the legendary Sopwith Camel aircraft than anyone else, one of which was involved in the demise of the great fighter pilot, Baron Von Richthofen, most commonly known as the Red Baron, who had declared that he lost his hunting instinct for about fifteen minutes after shooting down an Englishman. In 1936 aircraft production was transferred to Wolverhampton. A fine example of their fancy ironwork can be seen today in the metal fence surrounding St Peter Mancroft Church opposite the Forum (their name is on the gateposts).

The view of Norwich Cathedral and Lady Julian Bridge from the River Wensum

Carry on along the road – Wherry Road – and you will come to the new 'entertainment centre' of the city with pubs, clubs, a multiplex cinema and a bowling alley. You will also see the clean lines of the **Lady Julian Bridge** to your left. Walk across this, taking note of the wonderful views of Riverside on the left and the cathedral to your right. Walk straight up the path ahead until you come to **Dragon Hall** which is now the home of Writers' Centre Norwich. This magnificent medieval hall was built by Robert Toppes, referred to above. It fronts **King Street** which was once one of the most important streets in the city and centre of both commerce and the houses of the merchants who conducted the trade which made Norwich a wealthy city. Cross over King Street and carry straight on and up a narrow alley until you come to **St Julian's Church**, a small building to your left. Here you can enter the rebuilt cell in which Julian lived.

All shall be well, and all shall be well and all manner of things shall be well.

He said not 'Thou shalt not be tempested, thou shalt not be travailed, thou shalt not be dis-eased'; but he said, 'Thou shalt not be overcome.'

The greatest honour we can give Almighty God is to live gladly because of the knowledge of his love.

Lady Julian, Revelations of Divine Love.

Lady Julian was born about 1342, probably to a rich Norwich family, and died in 1416. Following a severe illness in the early 1370s, she received a series of visitations from Jesus Christ and meditated upon them for twenty years before writing a book, *The Revelations of Divine Love*, the first book in English by a woman, and one that has never been out of print since. Julian's meditations are remarkable and uplifting in the sense that she saw no anger or retribution in God's love as the quotes above, probably the most famous from the book, suggest.

There is a shop affiliated to the church that offers the chance to enrol in study groups.

Retrace your steps down the alley. Walk right along King Street to numbers 167 and 169. Here you have the **Music House**, now an educational centre, and the oldest secular building in Norwich. What you see is largely a seventeenth-century facade of a twelfth-century building. It has a stone-built undercroft with evidence of a brick spiral stair up and down. Records show that an early owner in 1225 was John Curry, who sold it to Isaac, son of a prominent member of the Jewish community, Jurnet the Jew. Twelfth-century features and sections, notably the North wing, are still there. Today it is Grade I listed and in the care of Norfolk County Council.

Re-cross the bridge until you come once again to the Riverside entertainment centre – a multiplex cinema is immediately ahead of you. Turn left and walk through the parade of restaurants and bars toward the station.

The walk continues across the very busy main road opposite **Thorpe Station**. This building, intentionally looking like an impressive country house, was built in the year following Queen Victoria's Golden Jubilee in 1887. Take the left-hand pavement and drop down to the river pathway below. You will soon come to Pull's Ferry again – on the other side of the river this time – and a few hundred yards farther along take the pathway leading down to the water. You will see memorial to a gruesome time in the form of a large tablet set into the grass and this commemorates the unfortunate souls who died in agony in **Lollards Pit,** the site of which is a little further along,

Norwich City skyline, featuring: Norwich Castle, City Hall, Norwich Cathedral and The Cathedral of St John the Baptist

almost opposite Bishop's Bridge. Many Christian martyrs, carrying their own bundles of firewood and preceded by chanting priests, were burned at the stake here. The records show that a woman, Cicely Orme, offered water to one of the burning men and was herself thrown onto the fire as a punishment.

One man who loved to walk around this area and up to Mousehold Heath was **George Borrow**, discussed above. **Mousehold Heath** can be reached by walking for a few minutes along and up the hill to your right. It affords fabulous views over the city, taking in all the major landmarks; it also has historical significance as just below here, in the Battle of Dussindale, Kett made his last stand in 1549 against the Earl of Warwick. The site was also

Bishops Bridge

cleared and became the testing ground for the Sopwith Camels and other
aircraft made by Boulton and Paul in the Great War. The impressive and
turreted redbrick building at the top of the hill is both a military barracks
and a prison.

A few yards down river from the commemorative tablet, providing a
pedestrian crossing point, is the beautiful **Bishops Bridge**, so-called because
it led directly to the Bishop's Palace. This is one of the oldest bridges in the
United Kingdom – we know it existed in 1249 as there are records of its
repair by the See at that date.

The Norwich Coat of Arms on Bishops Bridge

Bishops Bridge is etched into the Norwich mind alongside Kett's Rebellion, the most bloody episode in the city's history. As already mentioned, in 1549 the common man – with what historians see as quite reasonable grievances, including having their common land taken away by the nobility – found a champion in Robert Kett of Wymondham; 20,000 men assembled on Mousehold Heath. The king, insecure on his throne, was not best pleased and sent an army to crush the uprisers. In the ensuing battle, the **Earl of Warwick** took control of Bishop's Bridge. Kett's men attempted to cross it and enter the city to link up with their followers there. Wave after wave of Kett's men were killed. This bridge can look idyllic especially in spring when the daffodils on each side are in bloom, but it is a place where hundreds of Norwich men were cut down and killed. Eventually Kett retreated and his motley band was annihilated at the battle of Dussindale. Kett was hanged over the side of Norwich Castle, while nine of his senior lieutenants were hanged from an oak tree close to Wymondham called the **'Kett's Oak'**. Forty-five were taken to Norwich Market Cross and were hanged, drawn and quartered in the market area; 250 more were executed in whatever way pleased the victors, and this included being chained behind a horse which then galloped away over the famous Norwich cobbles.

Cross Bishop's Bridge and turn right following the river bank and you will come to **Cow Tower** which was a boom tower, as was the one earlier in this walk near Carrow Football Ground; here, monks would take a toll before allowing boats to continue up the river. It was built in the twelfth century and it has not had a top since Kett's rebellion when the Earl of Warwick blasted it off. Despite this it became what must have been a most terrible prison. If you go up to the iron gated entrance you can see how incredibly thick the walls are and that they are made of brick, a very expensive building material at the time. The tower was transferred to the city authorities at the end of the fourteenth century.

From here, continue along the footpath past the Adam and Eve pub on the left and St James' Mill on the right and you will come to **Fye Bridge** which links Tombland with Magdalen Street. In medieval times there was a ducking stool here to punish women for rowdy or drunken behaviour – men were treated separately, often being flogged, put into stocks or imprisoned without food or water in the Marketplace.

Robert Kett beneath the Oak of Reformation: an engraving by Samuel Wale. The Oak of Reformation was at the centre of the rebel camp at Mousehold Heath

'Kett's Oak', (not to be confused with the Oak of Reformation) situated on the B1172 road between Wymondham and Hethersett is said to be the meeting point for Kett's rebels

Cow Tower on a cold winter's day. Pretty daffodils cover this area in Spring

Fye Bridge from the River Wensum

If you like, turn left and enter Tombland where you will be almost where you started – the Cathedral Close is on the left. Alternatively, you can extend this walk by turning right and take a look at **Gurney Court**. This was the home of two remarkable women born to different families: Elizabeth Fry and Harriet Martineau.

Walk across Fye Bridge and into **Magdalen Street** where a short way along the road are numbers 31 to 35, a site bought by John Gurney, Fry's grandfather, in 1754. John died in 1770 leaving the property to his son, Richard who let his younger brother and Elizabeth Fry's father, John, rent it. John was a banker and established his business here. Elizabeth Fry's maternal grandmother was a Barclay and the two families merged in 1896, forming Barclays Bank as we know it today. There was a common saying at the time – 'as rich as the Gurneys' – which is quoted by Gilbert and Sullivan in *Trial by Jury.*

Folklore

Poor Sara of Magdalen Street

In 1860, 19 Magdalen Street was the scene of the murder by strangulation of Sara, who may have been in the attic of this public house with a man for, as the local papers put it at the time, 'an immoral and illegal purpose'. While the truth will never be known, many claim that Sara is still there. A succession of owners since then have witnessed slamming doors, cold, smoke, mirrors turned to face the wall and once, when occupied by a charity shop, a sack of clothes mysteriously sorting and folding themselves overnight; in the last case, the manager of the shop joked that he hoped she would stay and left more clothes out the next night, but Sara seems not to like to do the same thing twice. She has been seen hovering above what would once have been a flight of stairs. The Eastern Daily Press reported that one afternoon, when it had a life as a shop a customer sprinted, white-faced and shaken, from the back room and into the street, but unfortunately he could not be traced to find out what had scared him so. There have been attempts at exorcisms and several all-night vigils during one of which the sound equipment picked up a girl's voice saying possibly 'we know you'.

Born in 1780, Elizabeth Fry became widely known as a champion of prison reform, especially for women. She said: 'Punishment is not for revenge, but to lessen crime and reform the criminal.'

In 1801 the Gurneys left the Court for Earlham Hall – now the University of East Anglia's School of Law – and the Martineaus moved in; Harriet Martineau was 2 years old. She grew up to be a world-famous journalist and novelist, her most notable work being *Illustrations of Political Economy*, and she spent some time in the United States where she gained strong abolitionist views. In 1802 the Martineaus moved across the road to number 24 where there is a plaque, not, however, commemorating Harriet, but her brother James, a Unitarian preacher.

> The sum and substance of female education in America, as in England, is training women to consider marriage as the sole object in life, and to pretend that they do not think so.
>
> Harriet Martineau

The building itself had a chequered history thereafter, being sold by the Gurney family in 1811 only to have them buy it back in 1853. It was for a time called 'Grout's Court' and became an Agricultural School for Young Gentlemen followed by doctors' surgeries. In the early twentieth century shops were built at the front and more recently the interior of Gurney Court became flats and houses.

The walk can continue down **Magdalen Street** if you wish; it is a most interesting street full of eateries and shops, and although cut rudely across by a concrete flyover, it has a wealth of interesting features such as exquisite gables, windows, doors and foot-scrapers. At the time of writing there is much talk about rebuilding Anglia Shopping Centre which is situated just off the street to the left about half way down.

Alternatively, turn and walk back towards the cathedral. Just before you cross the river, on your right, is **Colegate**, well worth a walk down one side and back the other for some of the city's finest church architecture, meeting houses, industrial buildings and houses. It is notably home to the **Octagon Chapel**, built by Thomas Ivory in 1756. John Wesley said that it was so beautiful he was afraid people would stare at the features rather than concentrate on his preaching.

A few yards along is **St George Colegate,** built between 1460 and 1513, once quite wealthy and the place of worship of many city traders as well as one of the country's finest artists, John Crome, who has a fine marble memorial on the wall; he is buried in the south aisle. In the nave floor is set a tablet seeking vengeance for the death of a man called Bryant Lewis:

Portrait of John Crome, by Michael W. Sharpe

Here lyeth ye body of Mr Bryant Lewis
Who was barbarously murdered
On ye Heath near Thetford Sept 16 1698.
Fifteen wounds this stone veils from thine eyes
But reader hark! Their voice doth pierce the skies.
Vengeance cried Abel's blood gainst cursed Cain,
But better things spake Christ when he was slain.
Both, both cries Lewis gainst his barbarous foe
Blood Lord for Blood, but save his soul from woe.
Thou shalt do no murder – Exd XX 13.[8]

Turning right and crossing the river by the stone bridge at the end of Colegate you will find the Maids Head Hotel on your left. You will see the black surrounds of the 'Anguish Doorway' which celebrates a mayor of the town in 1611; Thomas Anguish was apparently fond of conducting business in the alehouse here and there are stories of his wife hauling him unwillingly out. He has a beautiful monument in nearby **St George Tombland** featuring

Elm Hill

himself with his wife and children, five of whom are carrying skulls – an indication that they predeceased him.

Opposite is possibly the most famous and most photographed street in the city – **Elm Hill**. This cobbled street has had several phases of life. In the thirteenth century it was a centre for the Black Friars (Friars de Sacco). In the fifteenth century it was a fashionable residential street and housed some of the Paston family. In Victorian times it fell into decay and council records show that in the early twentieth century it escaped complete demolition by a single vote. Today it is much loved by filmmakers.

The walk ends here; Tombland, where it began, is a few yards away so you have come full circle.

CHAPTER 2

Around the Coast

This chapter starts at King's Lynn and then proceeds in a clockwise direction around the Norfolk coastline.

King's Lynn

> Here are more gentry, and consequently is more gaiety in this town than in Yarmouth, or even in Norwich itself – the place abounding in very good company.
>
> Daniel Defoe, author *of Robinson Crusoe,* 1722[9]

In the Domesday Book of 1085 **Lynn** is described as a modest village. The word 'Lynn' may refer to the various pools and lakes in the area from which valuable salt was obtained. A town was begun by Herbert de Losinga from 1101 and he granted the residents the right to hold weekly markets. In 1204 **King John** granted the town certain rights and privileges in a royal charter and by 1350 Lynn was a large and important centre of about 6,000 people exporting salt, grain and wool. By 1500 it had become England's most important port. Just after this time one of the country's first water supplies was created using elm pipes under the streets – this could be linked to your house for a fee. A slow decline occurred thereafter although the town was still an important port, exporter of grain and industrial base, in particular, glassmaking and shipbuilding. Daniel Defoe, on his famous travels, considered Lynn to be 'beautiful' and the coming of the railways in 1847 provided a welcome boost. On 19 January 1915 the town was bombed by Zeppelins which had begun their journey at Great Yarmouth and followed the coast until inflicting extensive damage on King's Lynn during which two people were killed and several injured.

Lynn – a gruesome past

Lynn has a fairly grizzly reputation for immoral behaviour, crime and punishments in days gone by. A limerick which many local people know is:

There was a young lady of Lynn
Who was deep in original sin.
When they said 'Do be good!'
She said 'Would if I could!'
And straightway went at it again.

Hangings were common, as in all of Norfolk, in medieval times. Another form of execution here was the setting up of a cauldron of water with a fire lighted underneath. When the water was boiling, the felon would be dropped in. In 1531 in Lynn this was indeed done but, in addition, a gibbet with chain was placed above the cauldron. A girl servant, convicted of poisoning her mistress, was attached to the end of the chain and lowered in, then raised, then lowered again until her screams ceased.

As with some other areas of Britain in medieval times, King's Lynn was much concerned with witchcraft. The Corporation of Lynn invited Matthew Hopkins of Manningtree in Essex, rapidly gaining fame as the self-appointed and 'infallible' Witchfinder-General, to visit the town. In 1646 Dorothy Lee and Grace Wright were hanged for witchcraft, followed in 1650 by Dorothy Floyd, most probably on his advice. It is also on record that in Norwich, the esteemed Sir Thomas Browne attended, as an expert witness, two trials of women who were subsequently hanged for the same offence. As for Matthew Hopkins, it is said that he had his own 'infallible' tests set upon himself and failed them before being hanged in his turn.[10]

Deaths by hanging carried on for hundreds of years and the press reported them with gusto, sparing no details. On 28 September 1708, it was reported that a 7-year-old boy, Michael Hammond, and his 11-year-old sister Ann, were both hanged having stolen a loaf of bread. Another 7-year-old boy escaped death but was transported to Australia for stealing a pint of milk.

Public executions were big business all over Norfolk up to Victorian times, with crowds feasting, drinking, buying 'confessions' ostensibly written by the deceased, and holding a series of entertainments afterwards. Folklore suggested that women who could not conceive would have more luck in the future if they could 'touch' the body of an executed person, so bribery of those conducting the executions was rife.

A famous case, still the subject of discussion to this day, centres on a master at King Edward VII Grammar School in the town. He was apparently a very learned man who was, alas, hanged for murder in 1759. His name was Eugene Aram and, to this day, debate continues as to whether or not he was guilty. Although interest in the case has declined today, the British Library holds no less than ninety-seven books on the subject, mainly from the eighteenth and nineteenth centuries. Lord Edward Bulwer-Lytton[11] wrote a famous novel about him in 1832 and he became a Victorian cause célèbre. Aram was accused of murdering one Daniel Clark, who may or may not have been having an affair with Aram's wife, and with whom he was involved in a tawdry episode to do with stolen silver plate. In court he represented himself very eloquently, though evidently not eloquently enough, and many were the schoolboys where Eugene Aram had been a teacher who, in future years, took up his cause in a re-enactment of the complex case.[12] The proceedings would generally peak with an emotional recitation of his last written words in the early hours of the morning that he was hanged (he tells us that it was after 3 am because he had slept soundly until that hour):

Come, pleasing rest! eternal slumbers, fall!
Seal mine, that once must seal the eyes of all.
Calm and composed my soul her journey takes;
No guilt that troubles, and no heart that aches.
Adieu, thou sun! All bright, like her, arise!
Adieu, fair friends, and all that's good and wise!

Walk 4: A walk taking in the central part of King's Lynn

Distance: About two to three miles or longer if you decide to make an extended tour of The Walks at the beginning.

Time to allow: At least a complete morning or afternoon.

King's Lynn South East View, 1808 print

Walking conditions: Mainly level, although some of the ancient streets are a little higgledy-piggledy and uneven, with pavements on the narrow side. Wheelchairs can navigate the route but allowing some extra time is a good idea. The Tourist Information shop en route can provide ideas for other, more specialised explorations on another day. The Walks is a most beautiful place for a picnic. As ever, take a camera!

Walking visitors will discover a medieval gem. A good place to begin is around the **Purfleet Quay** and **South Quay** – if you are not too familiar with the area just ask for Saturday Market Place. Wandering around the surrounding jaggedly built streets, with some ancient houses having walls of deep ochre or blue, can be very interesting. In Queen Street you will discover **Thoresby College**, a magnificent sixteenth-century establishment for the training of clergy set around a courtyard (not open to visitors); in Nelson Street, **Hampton Court**, a merchant's house built in the fourteenth century; in Queen Street, **Clifton House** with twisting mahogany columns; and in St Margaret's Place, **Hanse House** which, as the name suggests, was once owned by the Hanse League of German merchants.

Back at the Saturday Market Place is **St Margaret's Church**. This lofty limestone structure was founded in 1095 by Herbert de Losinga who also founded Norwich Cathedral, and it housed a small priory of four monks who looked after his affairs in west Norfolk. The three-stage south west tower leans a fair bit as it was built on poor foundations from about 1260.

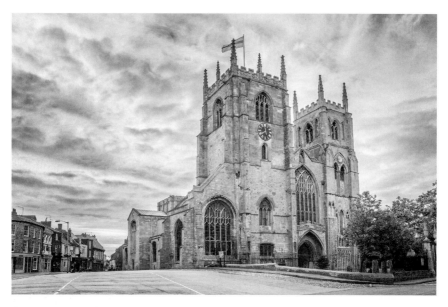

St Margaret's Church, King's Lynn

The church has seen various improvements, disasters (a spire blew off in 1741) and building works while Sir George Gilbert Scott oversaw a restoration in 1874 which brought very bright-coloured stained glass to the aisle windows. A leaflet is available in the church about these. In December 2011 it was dedicated by the Bishop of Norwich as King's Lynn Minster.

Opposite the church you will see the **Trinity Guildhall**, an imposing knapped flint and stone building. Venture up St James Street to find **Greyfriars Tower**, built in 1230 and important as a light to guide ships into port in medieval times. It is one of only three Franciscan monastery towers in England and is Grade I listed. It is noticeably leaning one degree to the west and is known locally as 'the leaning tower of Lynn'. At the end of St James Street is **The Walks**, a beautiful and extensive green on which sits the **Red Mount Chapel**. This is a fifteenth-century chapel for pilgrims on the way to Walsingham.

Return to St Margaret's Church again and walk up Queens Street where you will find the **Town House Museum** at number 46; this tells the social story of Lynn from medieval times by means of a series of rooms. Just afterwards, the street becomes King Street shortly before reaching what Nicholas Pevsner called 'one of the most perfect buildings ever built', the **Customs House**. This was designed by Henry Bell in 1685 and it sits in a waterfront square that is probably the most photographed scene in King's Lynn. Bell was a contemporary of Sir Christopher Wren and Mayor of the town. The Tourist Information shop is adjacent for queries. Here also are details of guided walking tours with the knowledgeable Red Badge Guides as well as leaflets suggesting self-guided walks. One excellent example of the latter is a Historic Lynn walk which traces the development of the town, as detailed above, from Herbert de Losinga's initial plans to the present day.

Carry on up Kings Street to **Tuesday Market Place** and here you will see another Henry Bell creation – the imposing **Dukes Head Hotel**. Once a very busy and important market, this extremely large site now has a small number of stalls in one part and a single shop – a chemist. It is primarily a car park at the time of writing, but does host a travelling funfair and large scale outdoor events throughout the year.

The Customs House, King's Lynn

Leave the marketplace from the top right-hand corner ahead of you and wander down St Nicholas Street to reach **St Nicholas Chapel**, the most extensive parochial chapel in England, begun in 1146 and much amended in the 1500s. This is truly spectacular, especially George Gilbert Scott's nineteenth-century spire and the wooden ceiling resplendent with angels.

Continue on and taking a left at St Ann's Street brings you to the quaint and worthwhile **True's Yard Fisherfolk Museum**. This is run by volunteers and features two beautifully restored Victorian fishermen's cottages plus a tearoom.

If you wish to go shopping, head back to the Tuesday Market Place and pass the Duke's Head Hotel on your left – this will lead you to the High Street and ultimately take you back to St Margaret's Church as you will be walking parallel to the streets (Kings and Queens) already travelled.

Elsewhere in King's Lynn

Everything to see in King's Lynn is within reasonable walking distance of the centre including **Lynn Museum,** which is a short distance from the shopping area, in Market Street. This has the life-size replica of **Seahenge** which is a prehistoric monument discovered at Holme-next-the-Sea in 1998. This was a timber circle, consisting of fifty-five split oaks with an upturned tree root in the centre, built in the Bronze Age. Scientists have discovered that the trees making up the circle were all felled in the same year which, incredibly, has been pinpointed as 2049 BC. Digital imaging has also been able to prove that exactly fifty-nine bronze axes were used in the shaping of the oaks. The locals had known of the feature for many years but it suddenly became a media sensation when a report appeared in the *Independent* newspaper. An outcry erupted and legal action threatened when it was proposed to move the timbers in the name of preservation, the *Eastern Daily Press* being furious as the 'whatever-it-was' (its purpose is still the subject of lively debate, although one theory is that it was connected to burials, especially so as Bronze Age pottery has been discovered nearby) belonged in Holme. It was, however, removed, treated, and rehoused in Lynn Museum.

Another older ring has been discovered 100 metres east and is known as **Holme II**. It predates Seahenge, dating from 2400 to 2030 BC and consists of two circles of oak logs surrounding a pit in which are two further oak logs. Perhaps mindful of the furore surrounding the removal of Holme I, this ring has been left to take its chances with the sea.

South of King's Lynn, the Fincham Hoard is a collection of Roman coins known as seattas which were in circulation from the last quarter of the seventh century and the first quarter of the eighth. Other rare seatta coins have been found in **Loddon** and **Aldborough** and all are the subject of current examination by scholars.

Notes and contact details

The Red Mount Chapel is open May to August with a small fee for entry. www.west-norfolk.gov.uk

For Lynn Museum and general information see www.museums.norfolk. gov.uk

True's Yard Fisherfolk Museum is open Tuesday to Saturday and there is a modest fee for entry www.truesyard.co.uk

Travelling on from King's Lynn

The A149 leads out of King's Lynn and across undulating countryside to Castle Rising. **Castle Rising Castle** with its massive surrounding earthworks was started in 1138 by William d'Albini for his new wife, the widow of Henry I, and is one of the most significant in England. In the fourteenth century it became the home of the infamous Queen Isabella, alleged instigator of Edward II's murder; local folklore has it that she can be seen sometimes prowling the battlements, unable to sleep out of guilt. The castle is owned today by Lord Howard of Rising. The whole site covers about 13 acres and consists of an inner bailey (enclosure) along with east and west outworks. In the early nineteenth century clearance work uncovered evidence of a church in the inner bailey slightly preceding the castle itself.

Also in the village is **St Lawrence Church** and the famous redbrick **Trinity Hospital** founded in 1614, which is for ladies who are required to be single, able to read, at least 56 years old, not a 'harlot', nor a 'frequenter

Castle Rising: Modern Day

Castle Rising: Eighteenth Century

of taverns' or a 'scold'. They still attend church every Sunday dressed in their scarlet cloaks on which is the badge of the hospital's founder, the Earl of Northampton. Once a year, on Founder's Day, they add a black steeple hat to their dress.

The A149 will lead you into Wolferton, the railway station of which was used by the Royal Family from 1862, which is when Queen Victoria bought Sandringham Estate for her son, Edward VII. It was closed in the 1960s – today the queen takes a car from King's Lynn station for her Christmas trips. **Sandringham Estate**, museum and gardens are open at quirky times, basically April to September – essential to check before you visit (see below). Sandringham makes a fantastic day out; a number of ground-floor rooms are packed with all sorts of royal trinkets and paraphernalia, including some of the gifts given to the queen from heads of state over fifty years. The gardens are beautiful and in the museum is a collection of vintage royal cars. **Sandringham Country Park** covers 600 acres with walking trails, play areas and a sculpture trail. Entry and parking is free and the magnificent grounds, with famous rhododendrons in hues of white, lilac, scarlet, pink, orange and lemon on display in May are free to visit. Dogs are allowed (though not on Sandringham Estate) if kept under close control.

Nearby is **Snettisham Park**, a haven for children with many farm animals to view including goats, chickens, sheep, as well as guinea pigs and a herd of deer. It is open February to mid-December and cost of entry is given on the website below. Snettisham is also arguably the most important site in England for viewing wading birds and pink geese as they cross here in their hundreds of thousands each year on a migratory odyssey. You can arrange to rise at the crack of dawn and join a party for breakfast while watching this great wildlife spectacle – details from **Snettisham RSPB Nature Reserve**, admission free.

The Snettisham Treasure is a collection of Iron Age metals found in 1948 and 1973. The find consists of seventy complete gold torcs – or torques – as well as 150 fragments. It has been suggested that this may well have been a royal Iceni collection. A further unrelated find was made in 1985 – a clay pot full of gold and silver from about AD 150. A hoard of Iron Age silver coins was also found nearby in **Fring** in 1993, 153 in total and all of the Iceni tribe.

The Reverend James Bulwer points to the supposed medical and magical power of torcs, the possession of which was, '... supposed to cause money laid by to increase, and they were specifics against poison from the bites of mad animals, and to abate the virulence of fever, and in cases of epilepsy'.[13]

In the mid-nineteenth century more gold torcs were found in Norfolk, two being at **Foulsham** and **Ashill**, near Watton, both of them being very similar. One was recorded at 33 inches in length; both could perhaps have belonged to Iceni chiefs.

Treasure Trove has always been an overwhelming interest to those in power. In medieval times, to hide the whereabouts of any gold you knew about was a capital offence. It is recorded that Henry VIII granted – i.e. sold – the licence to search for treasure in Norwich and Norfolk to a man called William Smith and his servant, who bribed various people to keep quiet when gold and treasure had been discovered and stole a great deal. When found out, the two bought some magic crystals and, hiding in woods, resorted to witchcraft to protect themselves from the wrath of the king; what happened to them after that has inspired many stories where it becomes impossible to separate fact and fiction.

The churches of Norfolk were also seen by the monarch as a source of income at certain times. In 1661, after the Restoration, Charles II was looking for additional income and ordered the sale of unnecessary furniture from churches including, we know from surviving records, St Andrews and St Mary Coslany in Norwich. It was an open secret, however, that the best pieces often did not make the sale as they were bought at hugely discounted prices by people of influence prior to the auction. The contemporary author, Peter Heylyn,[14] wrote in his *History of the Reformation* (1661):

And so it fared in the present business, there being some who were as much beforehand with the king's commissioners in embezzling the said plate, jewels, and other furnitures, as the commissioners did intend to be with the king, in keeping all or most part unto themselves ... So that although some profit was thereby raised to the king's exchequer, yet by far the greatest part of the prey came to other hands ... and many made carousing cups of the sacred chalices as once Belshazzar celebrated his drunken feast in the sanctified vessel of the temple.

St Mary's Church in Snettisham with its beautiful spire is often referred to as 'the Cathedral of West Norfolk'

An undated etching of St Mary's

A few miles away is Heacham, home of the famous lavender fields. In St Mary's Church is a memorial to Pocahontas who, in 1614 in Virginia, married John Rolfe of this village. She was the daughter of paramount chief Powhatan, and legend has it that in 1607 she saved the life of Englishman John Smith by placing her head on his when her father raised his war club for execution. She bore a son, Thomas Rolfe, in 1615 and travelled to London the following year where she was presented to society as an example of a 'civilised savage'. She died at Gravesend in 1617 aged about 21 and the whereabouts of her grave has not been determined for sure. Pocahontas is a legend, especially in America, and is the subject of an animated film by Walt Disney. Many people in America fancifully claim to be her descendent.

Hunstanton, just up the coast is unique in being England's only east-coast resort that faces west and you can see the sun setting over the sea. This is quite a thrilling spectacle and attracts many fans to 'Sunny Hunny' as it is known locally. The formal name is generally thought to derive from 'hun' meaning 'river', although there have been other interpretations, one of which gets short shrift from the great historian, Francis Blomefield:[15]

> Old authors derive the name of the town from Honey, as betokening sweetness and great might: the ancients were bad etymologists, and some of the moderns (it is to be feared) do not excel them.

Hunstanton's famous layered cliff rock

What draws people here primarily are the cliffs – layers of Norfolk carstone and red and white chalk dating to the Cretaceous period; you might find a fossil 135 million years old at their base. In this period many types of dinosaurs and pterosaurs roamed the country along with a growing number of birds. Mass-extinction followed called the Cretaceous–Paleogene extinction event, about 66 million years ago. There is speculation as to why this happened, one theory being the impact of an asteroid or increased volcanic activity which led to reduction in sunlight and hence photosynthesis.

Francis Blomefield, referred to above, writes of a local custom in the 1700s:

> Here, on certain great refluxes of the sea, called a dead neep, about the end of September, the inhabitants of the neighbouring villages can walk or ride, about 2 miles, to a place called the Oister-sea, where they take in their season, great quantities of oisters, some lobsters etc and indeed the shore abounds at all times with great variety of curious fish.

This is where Edmund, the first Patron Saint of England and ruler of the East Angles, landed. He can be found on the town sign and his extraordinary story is told in Chapter 4. It is also said that St Felix was approaching the coast in AD 630 in order to bring Christianity to the people of East Anglia when his ship was caught in a storm. The resident beavers came to his aid and in gratitude he granted the chief Episcopal status, and this is why the first Bishop of Norfolk is reputed to have been a beaver. This is celebrated today on the village sign of nearby Babingley which shows the beaver bishop. A fine statue of St Felix himself can be seen in the Anglican cathedral in Norwich.

Legends abound here and another tells the tale of King John who was making off with the crown jewels when they were lost overboard in a great storm – hence the original regal diamonds and rubies of England lie somewhere in the Wash.

Old Hunstanton has more recent claims to fame, one being that it was the location of **Hippisley Hut**, manned during the Great War by Bayntun Hippisley and his friend Edward Clarke. They were very early enthusiasts of wireless communication; Baytun Hippisley had intercepted calls of distress from the sinking Titanic in 1912. When war broke out, the government was very keen to utilise his skills and set him up in a wooden hut on the

Wreck of the trawler Sheraton on the beach at Hunstanton – she served in both world wars but was wrecked in a storm in 1947

Hunstanton cliffs; when dry, his team would go outside and set up their equipment exactly where people walk past the old lighthouse today. Interceptors like Bayntun were instrumental in many decisive actions of the war, including at the Battle of Jutland when the Admiralty knew exactly what the German navy was up to as a result of Bayntun's work. In the view of some historians, people like Baytun were instrumental in winning the war, although their actions were not widely known for many years afterwards. After the war Bayntun Hippisley returned to his home in Dorset and entered politics. He was awarded the CBE and died in 1952.

Hunstanton Lighthouse

New Hunstanton is a complete new town built by the celebrated Victorian architect, William Butterworth and funded by a consortium of businessmen led by Henry Styleman Le Strange. Built of mellow sandstone, it was begun in 1846 and a railway followed soon afterwards. It was mocked at first – the still-existing Golden Lion Hotel, originally called the Royal Hotel, was for a time referred to as 'Le Strange's Folly'. However, it proved a fantastic success; Rev Benjamin Armstrong, writing in his diary dated 20 July 1874, that was 'a complete fair, almost equal to the sands of Yarmouth in the height of the season…'.

The land on which the private Grade II listed moated house called **Old Hunstanton Hall** is situated has been in the possession of the Le Strange family since the time of William the Conqueror. In medieval times the locals were allowed on the land on Thursdays to gather firewood – at the time of writing this freedom of access still applies to walkers on this day, but best to check the current situation with Tourist Information.

Folklore

The Grey Lady of Hunstanton Hall

Dame Armine Le Strange lived in the Hall in the mid-eighteenth century, apparently in great splendour, her favourite possession being a carpet given to the family by the Shah of Persia. Her son Nicholas, a gambler, promised on her deathbed that he would never sell the carpet if he ever needed funds (which he constantly did) and, to keep his word, had the carpet put in a trunk which was stored in a far corner of the Hall, and entirely forgotten about.

A hundred years later, Hamon Le Strange took an American wife who started to renovate the Hall; exploring long-forgotten rooms she inevitably came upon a huge and dirty old carpet in a trunk. She decided to cut the carpet up and distribute it to the needy of Hunstanton. The hauntings started immediately and she soon realised that the figure she saw sadly staring was Dame Armine. The pieces of carpet were reclaimed and sewn together but it was of no use – the beauty of the carpet was lost forever. Dame Armine continues to stalk the corridors of the Hall, heartbroken about the fate of her beloved carpet.

The A149 soon heads into **Holme-next-the-Sea**. Many houses here and in the succeeding villages as you travel along the coast are built of a combination of clunch, carstone and flint. Clunch is a chalk from the Cretaceous age, between 154 and 66 million years ago. It sometimes has a greenish tinge, a result of the presence of iron aluminium silicate and potassium, and the rough texture is due to shell fossils. Containing high quantities of water it is easy to cut when excavated, but becomes harder as it dries out. It is used extensively in the interior of Ely Cathedral. Carstone is from the same period but is not suitable for carving or fine work; it is the chief building material of Sandringham House and very common at Hunstanton. Flint is found in buildings all over East Anglia but a particular form of flint, on the beaches here and along this coast, especially in the area of the Runtons, is known as Paramoudra flint or Potstone; the flint nodules have a hollow centre and resemble giant doughnuts.

Here also you will find great nature trails and a favourite site for butterfly and moth spotters. Holme has a unique claim to fame – as the 'moth capital' of England. Fossils of moths have been found that are 190 million years old while butterflies probably evolved from moths about 55 million years ago. Some 500 macro species and 400 micro species of moths have been recorded in the area, often blown here from the shores of Europe. Common varieties include the privet, poplar, and in summer, eyed hawk-moths. Some, like the bee-hawk or hummingbird moths feed while in flight, their wings beating at such a rate as to render them invisible. Other moths known to Norfolk have wondrous names – convolvulus, oleander, bedstraw, death's head, pale tussock, white satin, reed tassock, emperor and white ermine among them.

As regards Norfolk's butterflies, there is the spectacular black and yellow swallowtail which feeds on carrot and angelica, but especially likes milk parsley which is only found in the county. Its caterpillar is brilliant green with black stripes and orange spots. The metallic large copper is very rare and much more numerous are the common whites, clouded yellows and beautifully coloured painted ladies. The red admiral is common, too, although not exclusive to Norfolk's shores.

In 1965 the **Holmes Dunes National Nature Reserve** was created and now covers 550 acres. The dunes extend as far as the eye can see in places,

Holme Fen Nature Reserve

and it is possible to walk for long periods without seeing another person. Apart from moths, butterflies and birds – 382 species have been recorded hereabouts, common species being Brent geese, shore waders, chats, greenshanks and sea birds – the reserve is rich in plant life including marsh orchid and sea lavenders. In autumn the area becomes a mecca for the rapidly growing band of fungi-spotters and you can join a tour exploration party.

One of eleven Roman forts built to protect and control shipping around the coast was at **Branodunum**, near Brancaster. They were built in the third century and contained Roman garrisons for about 150 years until abandoned. The name Branodunum is derived from the local Celtic language and means 'fort of the raven'. Parking is available at Brancaster beach car park and then you can take a walk along the Norfolk Coast Path towards Brancaster Staithe. The site is basically a field with information board but the location is key. There are records to suggest that some of the walls still stood up to 12 ft high in the seventeenth century, but stones were taken to build elsewhere, including St Mary at Brancaster. The fort was subject of a 'Time Team' TV programme in 2013, prior to which excavations were conducted using ground-piercing radar and this led to unprecedented knowledge of streets and houses – contact the National Trust for fascinating details of this erstwhile community.

Notes and contact details

Castle Rising Castle is open all year round apart from 24–26 December, and it closes slightly earlier November to end of March. Entry is £4.50 for adults with reductions for concessions and children, plus there is a special family ticket www.castlerising.co.uk

Sandringham Estate and Sandringham Country Park, www.sandringhamestate.co.uk Tel: 01553 612908

Snettisham Park, www.snettishampark.co.uk Tel: 01485 542425

Snettisham RSPB Nature Reserve, www.rspb.org.uk Tel: 01485 542689

Hunstanton Tourist Information is in the Town Hall on the Green. It offers a leaflet with details of three walks for 50p. Tel: 01485 532610

The Coasthopper bus service is very popular along the North Norfolk coast, enabling people to walk in one direction and take the bus back. www.coasthopper.co.uk. Tel 01553 776980

National Trust, enquiries@nationaltrust.org.uk Tel 0344 800 1895

Thornham is next door and notable for the **Royal West Norfolk Golf Club** and the **RSPB Titchwell Marsh Nature Reserve**. A must-see is also the legendary and mysterious **Thornham Stumps**. Slightly inland are the villages that make up the Burnhams where you will find excellent local food and ales. In the thirteenth century the River Burn was navigable and these were ports, vital to the local economy. Burnham Thorpe is the birthplace of Horatio Nelson who, folklore has it, threw a party in the pub here before returning to sea in 1793. From Burnham Overy Staithe you can take a ferry or a number of cruises to see **Scolt Head Island** which is home to a number of nesting birds. There is a short nature trail here but much of the island is off-limits to protect the nesting areas. Just past Burnham Overy Staithe is Holkham Hall, owned by the Coke (pronounced 'Cook') family. The beach is vast and magnificent, not only for swimming and sandcastles, but for wildlife, birds and flowers.

Alongside Friar's Lane, off the B1355 in Burnham Market, can be seen the gorgeous fourteenth-century gatehouse, all that remains of the **Carmelite Friary of St Mary**. This was the first Carmelite house in England and was founded by Sir William Calthorpe in 1241. The order itself was relatively

The mysterious Thornham Stumps rise from the salt marshes

popular with locals because it seemed to have a genuine wish to preach the gospel and alleviate poverty – larger friaries were set up in Norwich, King's Lynn, Great Yarmouth and Thetford. Little is known about this particular friary as records have been lost, but it appears that seventeen monks were in residence in the sixteenth century. The site is open at any reasonable time and there is an interpretation panel at the entrance by the roadside.

Holkham Hall was started by the first Earl of Leicester and cost in total around £90,000, an amount so great that the family members were unable to modify the original designs as they wished and the result is that the house, seen as a severe and significant example of Palladianism, has remained much as it was when finished in 1764. Entry is through the Marble Hall – in fact pink Derbyshire alabaster – and a staircase leads to the state rooms, the most opulent of which is the saloon. The earls were concerned that each room should be symmetrical and sometimes this involved inserting false doors. Outside there is a 3,000 acre deer park, walled gardens, a mile-long lake, extensive walks, a Bygones Museum and History of Farming Exhibition which, much to children's' delight, includes tractors and old steam engines. There is also a shop.

The A149 carries on to Wells. Here you can take the Wells and Walsingham Light Railway which is the world's longest 10¼in in narrow-gauge steam railway. It takes travellers at a little over five miles per hour, with two stops en route, to the outskirts of Walsingham (see Chapter 3). At time of writing tickets are £9 per person, cash only. Carry along to Stiffkey and you can see the Elizabethan **Stiffkey Hall**, which is occasionally open to the public. It was begun in 1576 by Sir Nicholas Bacon, Keeper of the Great Seal; upon his death in 1579 Sir Nicholas left the house, along with £200 to develop the gardens, to his son Nathaniel, who was twice to become Sheriff of Norfolk and was

Warham Camp lies south of the village of Warham in Norfolk, hidden from the road in a field

knighted by King James. The house passed into many hands in the following centuries and was altered extensively. It remains privately owned today.

Warham Camp is an Iron Age fort near Wells, set off a pathway on agricultural land above the River Stiffkey. It is often talked of as a magical and evocative place with many wild plants such as common rock-rose,

Access to Warham Camp is gained through a gate on the side of the road

pyramidal orchid, quaking grass and squinancywort. Some observers have remarked on the specimens of Holm or Holly Oak which is an evergreen generally found in the Mediterranean – were the seeds or specimens brought over by wealthy young men returning from their continental 'tours'? It is the best earthwork in the region according to the University of East Anglia, with an overall diameter of over 230 yards and has outer and inner ditches and banks – some aerial photography suggests additional inner ditches. It would originally have been completely circular but is now horseshoe shaped due to the diversion of the River Stiffkey, which runs along a part of it, several hundred years ago. Wooden palisades would have given a 360 degree view of the surrounding land to occupants who could have included the Iceni. Iron Age and Roman pottery sherds have been found, although the central area of the fort has never been excavated; it may have later been reused by the Vikings. Access is any reasonable time and is free, although there is no proper parking and when the authors visited it was necessary to park a fair distance away, but the walk to the site was wonderful. It is a Site of Special Scientific Interest (SSSI).

At **Wighton**, south of Warham, seventeen Roman coins have been found – they are of copper alloy, of modest value and would have been used in everyday transactions for goods etc.

A barrow has been discovered about 1½ miles from Warham on the way to Binham. It is named **Fiddler's Hill barrow** and in 1933, before road widening, the skeletons of three humans and a dog were removed. Legend has it that the barrow is on the path of a tunnel from Blakeney to Binham Priory. The only person brave enough to enter the tunnel was a fiddler and his dog and this marks the spot where the devil took him as his fiddling stopped here and he and the dog were never seen again. The council planted apple and pear trees around the site after 2009 in order to encourage visitors and walkers.

At **Morston** is the tiny eleventh to thirteenth century church of All Saints. It does not have electricity, so services that take place there at night are by candlelight. You can take a boat tour from Morston or Blakeney – once bustling with trading ships – to see the grey seal colony.

Cley is famous for smoked seafood, wonderful walks, unique local ales and **Cley Marshes Nature Reserve**, from which you can walk to Salthouse

Cley Windmill

and join the **Salthouse Sculpture Trail**. You must not miss the much-photographed Cley Windmill – where you can also stay.

Cley is also famous as the village in which the poet Rupert Brooke was staying in 1914 at the outbreak of war. He was with Frances Cornford, granddaughter of Charles Darwin and she wrote of him:

A young Apollo, golden-haired,
Stands dreaming on the verge of strife,
Magnificently unprepared
For the long littleness of life.

Brooke was already a very famous young man and his untimely death during the war sealed his immortality, although he is not without his critics at the time or now. *The New Yorker*, in a commemorative piece on 23 April 2015, the hundredth anniversary of his death, describes him as '…holding on, to this day, to his fame and a rather tattered glory'. He died of blood poisoning having been bitten by a mosquito, but the government declared that he had succumbed to sunstroke – a more heroic image to suit the times. His most famous poem, 'The Soldier', was read out at his funeral in St Paul's Cathedral in April 1915.

> If I should die, think only this of me:
> That there's some corner of a foreign field
> That is forever England. There shall be
> In that rich earth a richer dust concealed:
> A dust whom England bore, shaped, made aware,
> Gave, once, her flowers to love, her ways to roam,
> A body of England's, breathing English air:
> Washed by the rivers, blest by suns of home.
>
> And think, this heart, all evil shed away
> A pulse in the eternal mind, no less
> Gives somewhere back the thoughts by England given;
> Her sights and sounds; dreams happy as her day;
> And laughter, learnt of friends; and gentleness,
> In hearts at peace, under an English heaven.

There is a Rupert Brooke society based in Norwich www.rupertbrooke.com

About five miles away is Weybourne – you can walk along the Norfolk Coast Path if you like or drive there in approximately 10 minutes. This is home to the Muckleburgh Collection. Opened in 1988, it is the largest private military museum in the United Kingdom, housing over 150 artillery pieces, tanks and vehicles, most of which are soundly maintained and working; it also houses the Suffolk and Norfolk Yeomanry Collection.

No less an authority than the Rev. Augustus Jessop DD, prolific nineteenth-century writer on historical matters and, according to some, eccentric country parson, believes that **Weybourne Priory** was founded before the Conquest. The monks, he writes, were not of the type just to retire from the wicked world solely to save their own souls but went out to help those oppressed. That they were busy and zealous, the writer believes, is shown by reports of how fine their church and priory became as 'the churches told tales – they will always tell tales'. The priory gained a visit from Bishop Goldwell in 1494, but was suppressed forty years later. The monks apparently had much time to prepare for the inevitable and when the commissioner came to value the goods and chattels, there was nothing left to take, except a haystack which was sold off for 66s 8d to Mr Thomas Pigeon. It was supposedly regarded as 'all fair play', and no recriminations resulted. Prior Bulman received a pension of £4 a year for

Weybourne Priory and All Saints Church

life and others, lesser amounts. Upon his visit to the site, Rev. Jessop is appalled at the ruinous state of the priory and church and he warns that if Weybourne wishes to once again become a thriving religious centre, those in charge must have energy and drive. He ends his heartfelt article by saying 'A dreary, God-forsaken place with only a crumbling ruin dedicated to the worship of the Most High can never, never, never, be a flourishing place of resort.'[16]

The remains of Weybourne Priory and tenth century Saxon tower

Sheringham traditionally gained its living from fishing and was a relatively unsung coastal village until the railways in 1887 transformed it into a major holiday resort from London and elsewhere for those keen to experience the healthy air. Hotels, shops and fine villas shot up with the cream of society wanting to be seen here. It was helped greatly by journalist Clement Scott, who was sent by his newspaper, *The Telegraph*, to write about its charms. He christened the area 'Poppyland' and it is still referred to as this today.

A famous resident of Sheringham was Olive Edis, often regarded as the country's first woman war photographer. She toured the battlefields in 1918 and worked on the photographs from her studio in Sheringham. Now, thanks to a grant from the European Union, her work has been digitised and can be seen today in Cromer Museum.

Mo Sheringham Museum, Lifeboat Plain, traces the town from fishing village to modern day resort. It has fabulous views from the café if you fancy tea or a snack.

Sheringham beach with traditional fishing boats

The famous Poppyline (North Norfolk Railway) operates from Sheringham Station – a complete station with waiting room, café and gift shop manned by liveried volunteers. A steam train will take you on a 20 minute trip in vintage carriages along a spectacular scenic route to the outskirts of Holt, where a bus completes the journey (at extra charge) to the centre of this busy market town.

The Runtons, East and West, are famous for traditional family holidays on sandy beaches. The cliffs are over 2 million years old in parts and a go-to area for fossil hunters, where finds originate from many mammals including rhinos and hyenas. Great excitement heralded the find in 1990 of what has become known as the **West Runton Mammoth**. Following a stormy night, two local residents, Harold and Margaret Hems, took a walk along the beach and saw what seemed to be a large bone sticking out from the cliff-face. The Norfolk Museum Service was informed. A year later, another local, Rob Sinclair, discovered more bones and in January 1992 the Norfolk Archaeological Unit began several years of investigations. Expertise from around the world became involved in what was obviously a find of major significance.

The Poppyline puffs through the North Norfolk Countryside on its way to Holt after departing from Sheringham

Previously, two examples of the skeleton of the species Mammuthus trogontherii had been uncovered, one in Germany and one in Russia, but they were only 10–15 per cent complete: this was 85 per cent whole. It would have stood 13 ft high, weighed 10 tonnes and it was male. It was taken to Gressenhall where some bones are on display, and also a few can be seen at Norwich Museum. Subsequent work at the Universities of York and Manchester managed to extract protein from the bones, a feat never before accomplished on remains over 600,000 years old.

Finds continue – in April 2017 the *Eastern Daily Press* reported that two amateur archaeologists had found the tibia of a mammoth that could be 2 million years old. This find was in the **West Runton Freshwater Bed**, a 5 ft thick layer of organic-rich mud deposited before the Ice Ages. It is believed to be full of fossils. As often, the find was made following storms when bones and fossils can be disturbed and consequently clues are sometimes visible on the land surface. Other finds recently have included part of (possibly) a mammoth jawbone and a tusk.

Mammoth partial scapula bone, found by the photographer of this book, Daniel Tink, who enjoys fossil hunting when not behind his camera. Found at Cart Gap on the East Norfolk coast, 2018. Length: 25cm

Mammoth tooth fragment, found by Daniel Tink at Happisburgh 2018

Other finds have included jet, amber and carnelian:

> During storms in the winter, jet can generally be found, and may have been washed out of the 'Forest-bed' as pieces have occasionally been found here. Amber is also obtained, but is much rarer, and large pieces are scarce. Carnelian are to be picked up in the shingle, but are of little use, the pieces being small.
> Savin's Geology of Cromer 1887.[17]

The best places for fossil hunting are Bacton to Cart Gap for mammoth and rhino remains; Hunstanton for sharks' teeth; Sheringham for fossilised coral; West Runton for belemnites and Sidestrand for fossilised fish. Check with the Visit East Anglia website below, or a museum if in doubt about anything you find or see and whether it is OK to take it away.

In this area can be seen basin-shaped depressions which were originally thought to be hut circles – pit dwellings of late Stone Age man. They are from 12 to 30 ft in diameter and from three to 6 ft deep, although a few have been discovered that are much deeper. Unfortunately, ploughing has completely obliterated a huge amount of evidence. Around Beeston, and also

Norfolk coast fossil finds by Daniel Tink. Top: Echinoid. Middle right: Echinoid. Middle left: Partial Ammonite. Bottom right: Jet. Bottom left: Belemnite

When visiting the Runtons during an exceptional low tide, you may spot on the beach (roughly half way between West and East Runton) 'Sharman Cutler's Stone'. It is believed that this large stone was initialled by a local stonemason from Cromer when it stood at the cliffs' base in 1770. The cliffs are now around 150 metres away, due to erosion

at Weybourne, there were many Victorian enthusiasts, often local vicars, who claimed to have found traces of fires once lit in the bottom of some; the theory continued that the roofs would have been made of branches and turfs. Modern thinking, however, tends to date them much later, to medieval times, and suggests they were shrieking pits which were formed by attempts to dig for iron-ore. The strange name may be because the disturbance of the gravels and subsequent incursions of water produced a 'shrieking' noise; others have proposed that mist or birdsong may be responsible for the strange sounds. Being Norfolk, there are also two ghostly legends that involve people 'shrieking'. In one, a distraught woman can sometimes be seen searching the pits for her new-born baby who was thrown into one by her jealous husband, convinced that the baby was not his. In the other, a 17-year-old girl called

Esmeralda jumped into one of the water-filled pits in despair at having been abandoned by her older, married lover, and it is her distressed cries that can be heard.

Below **Beeston Bump**, which is a relic of the Ice Age, is the site of the ruined abbey of St Mary in the Meadow, also known as Beeston Priory. Founded by Margery de Cressy the priory belonged to the Order of Peterstone, about which we know little, except that the monks were very outgoing, mixing and working with the local community. They ran a boys' school and were prosperous for a period, one of their privileges being the right to any booty or wreckage washed ashore on the nearby coast.

In 1317 Canon John de Walsam attacked the Bishop of Norwich during an argument and was sent to see the Pope who granted absolution. The south transept was ruined by flooding in the fifteenth century but the monks prospered until the abbey was closed and the goods looted by Henry VIII in 1540. This meant the school closed and it is believed that in 1555 Sir John Gresham founded nearby Gresham's School in Holt as a consequence.

The Priory of St Mary in the Meadow

The Priory of St Mary in the Meadow

In **Beeston Regis churchyard** there is reputedly an apparition dressed in grey who appears from behind the gravestones at sunset. One theory is that it is one of the monks who refused to leave when the abbey was abandoned.

Late Bronze Age finds have been made in this area – in Beeston Regis and Northrepps – including a number of socketed axes and pottery fragments.

Sheringham Park, Wood Farm, Upper Sheringham has over 1,000 acres of woodland and clifftop with wonderful rhododendrons and azaleas. Designed by Humphy Repton (1752–1818), it is two miles from Sheringham centre and has a visitor centre. Sheringham Hall itself is privately owned and not open to the general public.

Nearby Beeston Regis has something for the children – the **Priory Maze and Gardens** which is a quiz trail and hedge maze based around the layout of former Beeston Priory. An interesting fact is that, as you stand in the gardens which are on the east coast facing north, there is nothing between you and the north pole.

Before becoming fashionable, **Cromer** was described by a local guide in the early 1800s as being so quiet that it was 'a paradise for clergy and old ladies'.

Jane Austen subsequently declared it to be the best of all bathing places, while the *Eastern Daily Press* said: 'Cromer air has an extraordinary effect upon the digestive organs of those not accustomed to such a bracing climate, but that effect is of the most satisfactory and gratifying character.' As with the rest of the North Norfolk coast, Cromer boomed in Victorian times and many fine villas and hotels were constructed, including a rebuilding of the Hotel de Paris from 1871; the hotel is still open today. By the early Edwardian period Cromer prided itself on offering every delight and amenity for visitors:

'Many visitors delight in taking a walk along the cliffs to Trimingham, for, on mounting every successive eminence, the prospect commanded is beautiful.'

'Phaetons, sociables, and saddle-horses may be had of various job-masters, or at any of the hotels.'

'Hotel Omnibuses meet every train – the fare by which is sixpence to any part of the town.'

'A Visitors' List is published every Tuesday and Friday during the season, and may be obtained at 'The Library' or at the Post Office where names may be left for insertion.'

'Only those who have witnessed a fine sunset at Cromer can have any idea of its magnificence.'

All quotes from James Hooper, *The Illustrated Guide to Cromer and Neighbourhood,* Jarrold and Sons, London and Exchange Streets, 1902.

Today, it is a fine base from which to explore the area, having a variety of hotels, a tourist centre, excellent road, rail and bus transport links to Norwich, a good library, all manner of cafés – including some specialising in the famous Cromer crab – a bookshop (Jarrold), and it allows bathing, surfing and fantastic walks along the clifftops.

The **church of St Peter and St Paul** in the main street has the highest tower in the county with access to the top via 172 steps giving unparalleled views of the coast.

The striking war memorial at the front was completely renovated in 2018 and as a consequence it is easy to read the names of the dead carved upon it.

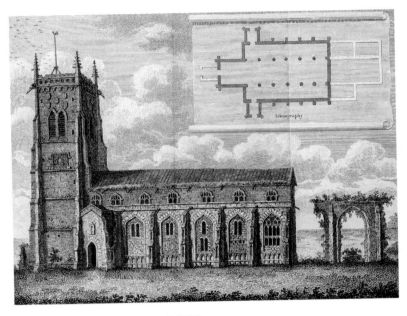

Church of St Peter and St Paul 1787

Church of St Peter and St Paul 2019

One of these is Alfred Lennox Fenner and there is a further memorial to him on a brass plaque inside the church. The son of a Cromer doctor, he was appointed lieutenant commander of HM Submarine *K4* at the age of 27, during the Great War. These new-fangled machines, largely developed in Norfolk, were unstable and unhealthy with an almost total lack of clean air and sanitation, and could blow up or sink with no notice. Lieutenant Commander Fenner, however, had a brilliant career and survived the hostilities, only to perish during peacetime activities off the Firth of Forth in 1918; it is believed that poor communications led to his submarine hitting a British trawler.[18]

Folklore

The Child in White

According to bestselling Edwardian writer James Hooper, there is a ghost here:

> If all be true that is said, a terrible ghost has been seen in the churchyard at Cromer. An old man working in the ruins of the ancient chancel, avowed that one evening he plainly saw the figure, it seemed, of a child clad in pure-white vestments, but it rose gradually til its face was level with that of the narrator, when, in a twinkling, a horrid gash broke across its throat, and a torrent of blood gushed over its bright garments. Then it vanished like a flash, leaving a long, sobbing sigh in the ears of the terrified spectator.

In the churchyard is a memorial with a striking epitaph. It commemorates Mary Allard, who died on 7 April, 1812:

29 years I liv'd a maid,
10 months I was a wife,
9 days I was a mother,
And then I lost my life.

Cromer Museum, next door, is devoted to fishing and has photos galore and some fossils.

Cromer Museum

Cromer's most celebrated son, 'one of the bravest men who ever lived', is Henry Blogg who, in both world wars, took his lifeboat out no matter what the circumstances, and saved 873 lives. In 1924 he was awarded the Empire Gallantry Medal; in 1927 a gold watch; in 1932 a silver medal, along with a second silver medal from the Canine Defence League because the rescue in question also involved saving a dog; in 1941 the British Empire Medal and at the same time his Empire Gallantry Medal was changed to a George Cross. When not manning the boats, he ran a business hiring out deckchairs. Henry died in 1954 at the age of 78. Today his sculpture sits on the top of the cliffs on North Lodge Park and in 2016, £10,000 was raised to place the hull of his crab fishing boat nearby. The **RNLI Henry Blogg Museum** on the Gangway (admission free) is dedicated to him; it has a café with views over the sea.

Today lifeboats are launched from **Cromer Pier**. Cromer has had a pretty disastrous relationship with piers – as has Hunstanton – until the latest one was built, opening in 1902 at a cost of £17,000. There are records of a pier in 1391 and a pier is also mentioned in a letter from Elizabeth I in 1582, but

Cromer Pier

these were washed away. A cast-iron construction in 1822 lasted twenty-four years before being destroyed in a storm. Norfolk County Council have kept the present pier well repaired and at Christmas 2018 it was selected by the BBC to pop up as an 'ident', which is a short visual image between programmes, over the holidays. Filming took place in October with hundreds of locals as extras.

Cromer is also famous in literary terms; it is the town from which Arthur Conan Doyle gained the idea for one of the best-loved Sherlock Holmes stories, *The Hound of the Baskervilles.* In 1901 he returned from South Africa where he had been collecting data for the British Government on the state of the army, which led in turn to a damning but practical report on how best to raise morale and health standards. It was this which led to his knighthood. He was, however, stricken badly with enteric fever upon his return and he chose Cromer as the place to recuperate. While here he learned the story of the 'Black Shuk', which locals believed roamed this coastline in search of its missing master (he died apparently in the 1700s) and would feast upon the throats of any locals he encountered after dark. Conan Doyle transferred the setting to Dartmoor, and his book was published to great acclaim in 1902, the year after his visit here:

And a dreadful thing from the cliffs did spring,
And its wild bark thrilled around.
His eyes had the glow of the fires below,
'Twas the form of the Spectre Hound.

Many locals firmly believe the hound to exist. Author Christopher Marlowe was taking a bicycle tour and passed through Cromer. Scoffing at the legend, he was challenged by some locals to spend a night in the area that was known to be haunted by the hound. He agreed and booked a room in a house nearby. When darkness fell he left the house and took up a good vantage point nearby. He saw the hound and:

> With a yell of terror I jumped up and fled. Not once did I look behind but I felt that the creature was in pursuit. Never have I run as I ran that night. Stumbling, cursing, breathing heavily, I tore up the lane and at last gained the threshold of the cottage … As the bolt was undone and the key turned I glanced around to see a pair of ferocious eyes fixed upon me and to feel on my neck a scorching breath. The hound was about to spring as the door opened and I fell fainting into the arms of my host.
>
> *People and Places in Marshland*,
> Christopher Marlowe 1927

Folklore

The Devil Dog of Shipden

The Spectre Hound, also called 'Black Shuk', is the most famous dog, but there is another also, which can be seen in the fading light on the beach looking out to sea. When it is approached it reputedly turns into vapour. Some claim its master lives in the sunken village of Shipden just beyond Cromer Pier, which at the time of the Domesday Book had 117 residents, and that the dog is pining for him. Others link the dog to a grisly Victorian tale suggesting that anyone getting into trouble in the sea here will be prevented from gaining the shore and safety by this 'devil dog'. There certainly has been a lot of drowning hereabouts. A tale in the local Cromer newspaper in 1860 claims that if you venture out to sea at a certain time and stay the boat over the sunken village you will hear the cries of men vainly trying to swim to shore, but being sucked downwards; it was at this time that Cromer Bay was labelled the 'Devil's Throat'. Some also claim that if you listen very carefully during a fierce storm, you will hear the jingling of the sunken church bells of Shipden as a ship goes down:

> Thick darkness broods on the churning deep,
> And shivers run thro' the night air;
> A blinding flash! Then a deaf'ning crash;
> Ah! What is revealed in the glare?
> With grinding shock on the great Church Rock
> An ill-fated vessel rebounds,
> And ever above the surging roar,
> A chime from the belfry resounds.

Felbrigg Hall is two miles from Cromer on the B1436. This Jacobean house, garden and estate was bequeathed to the National Trust by Robert Ketton-Cremer in 1969. The estate was originally owned by the Felbrigg family prior to the fifteenth century, and then owned by the Wyndhams for several hundred years. Inside you can see an array of eighteenth-century furniture and pictures and explore the Chinese bedroom. Outside, the 520 acre wood has several walking trails.

Gresham is a historically interesting village that lies five miles south-west of Cromer. It once had a square fourteenth-century castle: the moat and some ruins still remain. William Paston bought the manor of Gresham from Thomas Chaucer and it was fortified in 1319. The ownership of the manor was heavily contested by both legal and armed means until the manor was sold to the Batt family in 1620 who have owned it ever since.

Notes and contact details

Holkham Hall is on the A149 and the Coasthopper bus stops at Holkham, which is three-quarters of a mile from the Hall. King's Lynn railway station is twenty-three miles away. Bike storage is available for cyclists. It is open March to October. Visitor Enquiries/Ticket Office: visitorinformation@ holkham.co.uk Tel: 01328 713111

Salthouse Sculpture Trail, www.salthousetrail.co.uk

Cley Windmill, www.cleymill.co.uk Tel: 01263 740209

Wells and Walsingham Light Railway, www.wellswalsinghamrailway.
co.uk Tel: 01328 711630

Warham Camp, www.norfolkcoastaonb.org.uk

Priory Maze and Gardens, www.priorymazegardens.co.uk
Tel: 01263 822986. Open Wednesday to Sunday 10.00 am – 3.30 pm.

Mo Sheringham Museum, www.sheringhammuseum.co.uk
Tel: 01263 824482

Hillside Animal and Shire Horse Sanctuary, West Runton, www.
hillside.org.uk Tel: 01263 837339.

Sheringham Park, sheringhampark@nationaltrust.org.uk
Tel: 01263 3820550

Poppyline Train times vary so best to check in advance, www.
nnrailway.co.uk Tel: 01263 820800

Fossil hunting, www.visiteastofengland.com Tel: 0333 320 4202

Cromer Museum, www.museums.norfolk.gov.uk Tel 01623 513543

Cromer Pier, www.cromerpier.co.uk The Pavilion Theatre hosts variety
shows all summer.

Felbrigg Hall, www.nationaltrust.org.uk Tel: 01263 837444

Just beyond Cromer is many people's idea of the ideal Norfolk coastal village –
Overstrand which has three Edwin Lutyens buildings and a marvellous
beach; often visitors will not venture beyond Cromer as public transport is
erratic (there is no railway any more) and turn back towards Sheringham, or
head inland to Norwich. You can, however, continue all the way to Hopton-on-
Sea on foot if you have the energy and be rewarded with spectacular views.

Six miles away, **Mundesley** is fairly quiet today but was once part of the
fashionable coastline so beloved of Victorians.

And the cliff is so irregular, with many slips, foreshores, patches of grass and
coltsfoot, and slopes of grey, red and yellow, and a grassy undercliff with a
pond in the hollow, and a marly bluff, and gullies and chines, so as to look
strikingly picturesque.

William Cowper (see under Dereham, Chapter 3)
describing Mundesley in a letter.

Mundesley appeared in the Domesday Book of 1086 when it was variously known as 'Muselai' or 'Muleslai'. The name is likely to derive from the fact that the village of Mundesley is the final outlet point for the river Mun. Therefore the name of the river is conjoined with the word 'leah', which itself usually means 'a clearing' or 'open ground'.

The population of the village has grown very slowly since its first formation as a very small cluster of dwellings, likely to have been only single storey simple huts. In the fourteenth century there were less than twenty dwellings. By the 1841 census, the population had reached 455.

Things changed radically when the railway arrived in Mundesley on 1 July 1898. The stylish station was designed and built with no less than three 600 ft platforms. That's a lot for a small town. In the initial years the station saw sixteen trains arrive from North Walsham and beyond every day. In 1903 the large sum of £93,000 was invested in extending the line from Mundesley to Cromer, but fifty years later the line was closed. Dr Beeching, who in 1961 became Chairman of the British Railways Board and produced a report, 'The Reshaping of British Railways', ended the railway altogether. Part of the old rail track route is now a public walking area, known as **Pigney's Wood**, where visitors can find, among forty species of tree, a 450-year-old oak.

Present-day Mundesley has a population of approximately 2,700. In its late nineteenth-century heyday Mundesley, like its neighbour Cromer, became such a fashionable summer coastal resort that no less than three new hotels were built to accommodate everyone. The Clarence opened in 1891 and The Grand and The Manor hotels took their first guests in 1897. Prior to this there was only one hotel, The Royal, which is an old building with its origins probably dating back to the early seventeenth century.

A little less than two miles further along the coast is Knapton. The **church of St Peter and St Paul** is beautiful. On entering, look up and there above you, on well over 100 pairs of angels' wings, hovers the most intricately carved roof of any church in Norfolk. John Smithe gifted this creation to the church in 1503. It has been said that on occasion, even the carved wooden eagle's head on the readers' lectern standing in the nave cannot resist twisting its neck up to look in admiration at the beauty above.

The interior of St Peter and St Paul Church, Knapton

Close up of a wooden angel in St Peter and St Paul Church, Knapton

The church of All Saints is to the north of the village. A church standing within 12 acres of land is mentioned in the Domesday Book of 1086, but the structure of the present church is mainly of late fourteenth century origin. In 1844, after years of neglect, it was decided to increase the size of the building, and an extension was built at the west end of the nave and a gallery inserted, which survives today. In 1903 the church was extended again and further work was completed in 1914.

Epitaph spotters have a rewarding time in rural Norfolk – they range from the profound to the quirky and crazy; many articles and even books have been written about them. Here is one which is well known locally, taken from St Botolph's Church, Trunch, about a mile inland from Mundesley and quoted in *East Anglian Epitaphs*, R. Lamont-Brown (Acorn Editions 1981).

Here lies Fred, who was alive, and is dead.
Had it been his father, I had much rather:
Had it been his mother, better than another:
Had it been his sister, no one would have missed her:

The Mundesley Maritime Museum built in 1928

Had it been his entire generation,
So much better for the nation:
But since 'tis Fred, who was alive, and is dead,
There's no more to be said.

Mundesley can arguably claim to have one of the smallest museums in the world. It is housed in the ground floor area of what was the old Coastguard Lookout Room, perched near the clifftop, on the pretty lawned area on Beach Road. It is certainly worth a visit to see lifeguard and general maritime paraphernalia.

Between here and Happisburgh, on the edge of Bacton village, lie the ruins of Bromholme or **Broomholme Priory**, founded in 1113 by the Cluniac order. It became very wealthy, the taxation returns of 1291 showing that it owned property in fifty-six Norfolk, and sixteen Suffolk parishes and had an annual valuation of £106 15s 11d.[19] There were twenty-five monks resident at this time. In 1223 a cross, reputedly made from fragments of the true cross, was acquired from Hugh, a Norfolk priest, who claimed to have carried it from the deathbed of the Emperor of Constantinople. Pilgrims flocked to witness reported scenes of miracles that included the raising of the dead. We know a great deal about the history partly because the priory had much to do with the Pastons, was generously endowed by them and is mentioned in their famous letters, as it also was by Chaucer in the *Reeve's Tale*. John Paston was buried here in 1466.[20] Thousands of finds have been made in the area. The priory ruins are on private land now, which is sometimes open to the public.

In St Margaret's Church, Paston village, can be seen an extraordinary monument to 'the vertuous and right worthy dame', Lady Katherine Paston, executed in 1629 by Nathaniel Stone at a cost of £340.

One mile to the north of Bacton is a small motte and bailey known as **Newport Tump**, which was probably abandoned in the fourteenth century.

A little farther round the coast is **Happisburgh** (pronounced 'Haisbro') which offers exhilarating walks along the crumbling cliffs. The modern settlement has a population of about 1,400 people living in 600 households, according to the 2001 census. Some houses date back to the sixteenth century. The land around the village, of a rich friable loam, is considered to be of a very high farming quality and produces Wheat, Barley, Turnips, Swedes and Beans. To a declining extent, fishing also produces income and work for local people.

The oldest ever human European footprints were found here in 2013, left in solidified mud and believed to be 800,000 years old. Investigations are ongoing.

Just below the church in Happisburgh you will find a fine and unusual village sign depicting some prominent villagers: Edric the Dane – owner of the land before 1066; Maud, daughter of later landowner, Roger Bigod; and the Rev. Thomas Lloyd who held a mass baptism of 170 poor folk in 1793, thus saving them the expense of the party that was expected to follow individual baptisms.

There have been many disasters at sea. A terrible storm in 1692 caught over 200 ships sailing between Wells and Winterton. Perhaps 1,000 men perished in one night. On 19 December 1770, HMS *Peggy* foundered on the shore in a NNE squall. Many brave villagers brought carts and horses

Hand axe, Lower Palaeolithic, 600,000 years old (Wymer type D) found at Bacton by John Crann in 2018

onto the beach at low water the next day and managed to bring fifty-nine men safely ashore. Alas, thirty-six more were buried in the local churchyard.

The largest ship to be lost off the coast hereabouts was HMS *Invincible* on Monday 16 March 1801. She was laden with stores and 600 men and on her way to join Admiral Nelson prior to what was to become the Battle of Copenhagen. She ran aground a sandbank off Happisburgh and subsequently sank. Heroic efforts in dreadful conditions saved 190 men but as many as

400 were lost, including the captain, John Rennie; many bodies were washed-up on the coastline in the ensuing days and 119 men were hastily buried in a mass grave, evidence of which was discovered during excavations in 1988. Later that year, they were at long last given a Christian burial, in the presence of a descendant of Captain Rennie and eight serving members of the modern-day aircraft carrier *Invincible*.

Folklore

The ghost with a severed head and no legs

A legendary tale takes us back to around the year 1800. Three sailors-cum-smugglers fell out with each other over the amount of money they were going to share after selling illegal brandy to the locals. Drinking heavily, they fought and one was killed. The body was dropped down a nearby well.

Not long afterwards a Happisburgh man, Sydney Baker, had been having a few beers at the Hill House pub, and was staggering down the slope back to the village. Moving towards him from the direction of the sea appeared to be a man with no legs and his head dangling behind him, carrying a sack. Sydney struggled home but the next night he went with four friends to the well at midnight and the same apparition appeared. Next day the well was found to contain a torso and a sack containing a pair of legs and a head.

The site of the now filled-in well can still be visited about three quarters of a mile along the B1159 coastal road heading out of the village towards Whimpwell Green.

Happisburgh inspired Sir Arthur Conan Doyle in one of his famous Sherlock Holmes stories. He came here on a motoring holiday in 1900 and lodged in the Hill House Hotel. The landlord's son, Gilbert Cubitt, had devised a way of writing his signature using miniature 'pin men' and this so intrigued Conan Doyle that he weaved it into his story *The Dancing Men*, which was set in and around this part of Norfolk. Interested visitors will find a good deal of Conan Doyle memorabilia here.

Happisburgh Lighthouse

Happisburgh's most famous landmark is the lighthouse, which, with its 85 ft tower and red and white 'hoops', has served since 1790. Once there was a sister tower 20 ft lower, but by 1883 coastal erosion hurried on the task of dismantling it before the sea did the job anyhow. The night-time beam

A surviving Pill Box at Happisburgh (probably from the Second World War, although it is not always possible to be certain as those from the Great War were sometimes adapted and reused)

identification is three white light flashes, repeated every thirty seconds. Manned entirely by volunteers, the public – subject to a height restriction – can climb its 112 steps on about a dozen occasions during the year.

Happisburgh can also boast a volunteer Coast Watch Station, positioned on the cliff top. It is manned every day of the year and has a sweeping view of about ten miles of horizon and sea. It reports to HM Coastguard at Great Yarmouth.

Another dedicated team will be found at the Happisburgh inshore lifeboat station at **Cart Gap,** which is run under the auspices of the Royal National Lifeboat Institution. It relocated in 2002 due to a serious cliff-fall and can now be found at Old Cart Gap.

The splendidly poised and imposing structure of the 110 ft high tower of the **church of St Mary** draws your eye, even when you are still not within a mile of Happisburgh. It has stood here since the fifteenth century. Sir John Betjeman loved what he saw, and couldn't resist remarking that the tower was slightly out of alignment with the body of the church itself. Nevertheless, it is seen by many as one of the finest in a county of wonderful churches. The font is fifteenth-century craftsmanship of great beauty. The church itself fell into sad disrepair in the nineteenth century and extensive remodelling took place, including a completely retimbered roof of red deal. Work has been continuous since then. Donations towards the upkeep of this coastal cathedral, via the Restoration Fund gift box, are always most gratefully received. Visitors can climb to the top of the tower, which is open regularly during summer months. There are 133 steps to the top from where, on a clear day, you can see Norwich Cathedral spire, some eighteen miles distant.

In mid-2010, the BBC announced some results from a six year excavation on Happisburgh beach. Of international significance, it suggests that man occupied these parts much earlier than previously thought – maybe 970,000 years ago. This was a species of man that has since died out; similar to us, but maybe with a flatter face, not much of a chin to speak of and larger teeth. Further research is ongoing.

Folklore

The witch of East Somerton

St Mary's Church, East Somerton, is famous for having a large oak tree growing in the nave of the ruined structure. Built in the fifteenth century, it was abandoned in the seventeenth and local legend has it that vengeful locals buried a witch alive here – she had a wooden leg and it is this which grew and destroyed the fabric of the building. It is said that if you walk around the tree three times, the vengeful spirit of the witch will appear (this is a common way to summon spirits in Norfolk; for example, it is said that if you walk three times around a 'pingo' – a pond formed in the ice age – along the Peddars Way at midnight, the Devil will appear).

For an interesting detour, take the B1145 from Mundesley and explore the market town of **North Walsham** (it is also on the direct rail line from Norwich). In the twelfth century this town became very prosperous with the

Flint core. Lower Palaeolithic, 600,000 years old found in 2019 by Daniel Tink, photographer for this book. A flint core was a striking platform used with a hammerstone for detaching small razor sharp pieces known as flakes, used for cutting. The core was often discarded, or crafted further into a tool such as a hand-axe

arrival of weavers from Flanders – today 'Walsham' is the name of a lightweight cloth for wearing on hot days. It has an exquisite village pond, much loved by photographers. The **church of St Nicholas** was very fine, having the second tallest spire in Norfolk until it collapsed in 1724. Various attempts to rebuild it over the centuries have come to nothing; now the ruined tower dominates the town. Inside is the elaborate tomb of Sir William Paston who founded Paston Grammar School in 1606 at which Horatio Nelson studied for a time. This was just after the Great Fire of 25 June 1600, when a blaze originating in a private house occupied by a man named Dowle – who ran off but was captured and clapped in irons – destroyed over 100 houses, seventy shops and the market cross.

The town is home to the **Norfolk Motorcycle Museum** which, apart from eighty motorcycles, also houses a collection of diecast toys. **Stow Mill** at Paston is a traditional Norfolk flour mill built in the 1820s where you can

The church ruins of St Mary's, East Somerton, with its mysterious oak

climb on ladders to the shop right at the top. **Paston Way** begins here and you can walk the twenty miles to Cromer taking in fifteen churches and villages along the way. Overall, here is an ideal base for exploring both the coast and the inland villages like **Trimingham, Trunch, Knapton** and **Northrepps**. Trimingham was famed in the middle ages as it was claimed that the head of John the Baptist had found its way to the parish church. Northrepps is noted for developing a type of plough – the Gallus plough – used for 100 years from 1830, and the village was a centre for smuggling. **Beacon Hill**, the highest peak of the Cromer Ridge at 338 ft, is a mile from Trimingham. There are various hotels as can be expected but also some excellent holiday cottages.

Trimingham, Gimingham, Knapton, and Trunch, Southrepps and Northrepps, lie all in a bunch.

Local saying

Folklore

Challenging the Devil

Sea Palling has Norfolk's biggest barn at 180 ft long, built about 1570 – **Waxham Hall and Great Barn**, Sea Palling. The Great Barn is the largest in the county and is open to the public. In the 1770s it was owned by Sir Berney Brograve along with the manors of Horsey and Sea Palling, and a mill called Brograve's Mill. Legend has it that Sir Berney made a bet with the Devil that he could out-mow him over two acres of bean plants, and that if he lost he would give up his soul. He duly lost and retreated to the mill, where he barricaded himself in as the Devil tried to bash the door down with his cloven feet. The mill is now abandoned.

South of Horsey is the **Horsey Windpump and Mere**. This is a five-storey drainage windpump and, after checking out the interior, there is a three-mile circular walking trail to try.

At **Caister-on-Sea**, on the western edge of the town, lies **Caister Roman Site**, the remains of a Saxon Shore Fort built around AD 200 and occupied

Waxham Great Barn

until probably AD 390. You can wander around the 8.6 acres and clearly see the ruined walls of a square building. There would have been towers at each corner and, as is often the case with Roman forts in Norfolk, a fortified gate in each side. There are a series of rooms of differing sizes and in at least one – the second room from the west – can be seen evidence of Roman central heating in the form of a Hypocaust heated floor. Entrance to the site is free.

A short distance away and off the A149 is a partial building to explore – **Caister Castle**. The 100 ft tower is all that remains but can be climbed by visitors. Originally, this was part of an imposing house constructed by Sir John Fastolf – some say the inspiration behind Shakespeare's Sir John Falstaff – between 1432 and 1446. It suffered damage when attacked by the Duke of Norfolk in 1469, and largely fell into ruin after 1600. Like many other projects, both big and small by wealthy people in medieval times, the building was designed to be somewhere that people could pray for Sir John's soul in perpetuity. Alas, this did not occur for long because the castle was claimed by the Paston family – and features in the Paston Letters[21] – to whom it eventually passed after bitter disputes including a two-month siege. **The Caister Castle Motor Museum** is on the same site.

Caister Castle

Medieval pottery and alloy finds have been made at nearby **Mautby**. Margaret Paston, one of the writers of the Paston Letters, lies here. (One hundred letters, sent to her lawyer husband when he was away on business, have survived.) When she died in 1484 aged 60, she was buried at her request in the church of St Peter and St Paul but, as the church subsequently fell into neglect and records were lost, exactly where is a matter of conjecture.

Great Yarmouth adjoins Caister and has long claimed to be East Anglia's premier holiday resort and the jewel in its crown is undoubtedly the glorious beaches of golden sand, rivalling Suffolk's Lowestoft in this regard. There is everything you would expect to be here and to do in a seaside town – buckets and spades, paddles in the sea, greasy spoons, gift emporiums, crazy golf, a shop where you can see rock (the edible kind) being made and rolled out, fast food, and rides along the extensive prom in horse-drawn carriages. Originally very prosperous partly because of the herring – these so-called 'silver darlings' were a valid currency and sent to London for the monarch in part-payment of taxes – and beloved by the Victorians, it suffered a decline in fortunes in the twentieth century and was bombed in both world wars.

> I have lived in Norfolk all my life. It inspires me, the sea, the limitless skies, the mud and the burning sunsets and the freedom of a place where 50% of the neighbours are fish.
>
> Raphaella Barker

In the Middle Ages Yarmouth was Norfolk's richest, and England's fifth richest, town. In an essay written in 1907 for *Norfolk Archaeology*, Rev. William Hudson FSA found that a tax assessment for all Norfolk towns was made for Edward III in 1334. In it Norwich, the second most prosperous settlement, was given an assessment of £94 12*s*, but in top place was Yarmouth at £100. He doubts, however, if this was actually ever paid as it was during this period that the source of Yarmouth's great wealth, the harbour, began to be blocked by sea-driven sands and there are records of Yarmouth petitioning the king against such a high 'valuation'.

Great Yarmouth has some of the best conserved medieval town walls in England. Because Yarmouth was an important port, on 28 September 1261 King Henry III granted the right to build a defensive wall with a ditch – it took over 100 years to complete; large sections and eleven towers remain today. One of the towers – the South East Tower in Blackfriars Road – has undergone a £100,000 renovation and is available to rent for holidays, sleeping six. It is run by the Great Yarmouth Preservation Trust and it is possible, subject to funding, that others may be similarly converted.

A stretch of Great Yarmouth's medieval town wall with the South East Tower

A close-up of the South East Tower

Walk 5: A walk around Great Yarmouth

Distance: About four miles. The seafront continues for miles and so this walk can be extended almost as much as you like.

Time to allow: A complete day: it is almost inevitable that you will discover shops, streets, and parts of the seafront that deserve an extra look.

Walking conditions: Flat and easy going. Wheelchair users will experience few problems except possibly if using the shopping centre or bus station which can seem cramped and busy at peak hours. There are numerous places to eat and drink on the route: despite this, the street distances are long and it can get surprisingly hot as you walk so best to carry a drink with you. Take a camera!

This walk starts at **St Nicholas Church**, which is the first imposing building you will see if driving in from Norwich. It is also not far from the train station. If coming by bus, alight at the bus station and cut through the market square – less than ten minutes' stroll.

Claiming to be the largest parish church in England, it is now without a spire as this was lost in a bombing raid of 1942, after which the church interior was rebuilt. The minster is very welcoming and has details and old photographs of its history on the walls, one example of which shows Victorian fishermen dragging their nets into the church for blessing. As you enter on the right, in the porch is a window dedicated to the Norfolk Regiment (before it became 'Royal'). It can take an hour or more to wander around, there are toilets and sometimes a café is open for tea and biscuits.

The church became embroiled in a body-snatching scandal in 1827 when two men were hired by Sir Astley Cooper, surgeon to George IV, to find bodies for medical experiments, which they did by raiding twenty graves in St Nicholas churchyard. They were crated up and sent to Sir Astley in London, the crates being marked 'Glass – handle with care'. Before being sent to London: they were held in Row 6, Great Yarmouth, which became known as 'Snatchbody Row'. An ironic fact is that Sir Astley's father had been vicar of St Nicholas Church. The main local organiser, a Beccles man called Thomas Vaughan, was subsequently transported to Australia for body-snatching but the authorities were unable to trace the events directly to Sir Astley. Body-snatching was very profitable, if illegal, and carried on for the whole Victorian period.

From the fifteenth century it was the custom of the dean and chapter of St Nicholas, along with their farmer, to provide a Christmas Day breakfast for the needy inhabitants of the town. Francis Blomefield, in his *Topographical history of the county of Norfolk, etc.*, writes that in the mid-sixteenth century, William Gostlinge, the farmer on whose land the breakfast (a slice of bread and meat washed down with some beer) took place, refused to give it for various reasons, one being that it profaned the name of Christ because participants would proceed to get drunk all day 'until eleven of the clock'. His main argument against it, however, was put to the councillors of Yarmouth in these words:

> In regard of the danger of gathering together of at least a thousand people, the most party of them being of the rudest and basest sort, all which meeting, there hath been oftentimes danger of a murther [murder], by quarrelling and fighting among themselves, and also a breaking of windows, tables, stools, pots, glasses, and many other disorders, which can by no means be prevented.

The council ruled that the breakfasts should be resumed but the farmer refused; the impasse went on for many years until eventually resolved by farmer Gostlinge's son who, having taken over the farm, agreed to donate £10 a year to the relief of poor fishermen in place of future breakfasts, along with a one-off fine of £5 for the cancellation of the Christmas tradition without the council's authorisation.

Anna Sewell and *Black Beauty*

As you leave by the main gates, look left to see a striking little cottage, the birthplace of Anna Sewell (30 March 1820 – 25 April 1878), author of just one book – but one which has sold over 50 million copies – *Black Beauty*. The full title page reads: *Black Beauty: His Grooms and Companions. The Autobiography of a Horse. Translated from the original Equine by Anna Sewell*. It has become one of the most influential books of all time, the forerunner of the 'Pony' books, but it was not Anna Sewell's intention that the book should be for children – rather it was intended to promote kindness towards horses by adults. She completed the manuscript while living in the

Catton area of Norwich and it was taken up by Jarrolds of Norwich, who ran a printing business. It was published in 1877 and Anna was able to witness the beginning of its incredible success before she died.

When she was 14, Anna had badly damaged her ankles in a fall when walking home from school, and for the rest of her life was an invalid. She loved to drive her father to and from his work in a trap and it was this that gave her a love of horses. Literary success ran in the family; her mother, Mary Wright Sewell, was a very successful writer of tales for young people. In 1865 she published *Mother's Last Words*, a tale of how two boys are saved from sin by their mother's final words – it has since sold over a million copies. Her other works include *Our Father's Care: a Ballad* (1857) *and Ballads for Children* (1867).

Anna was bedridden and in considerable discomfort when writing *Black Beauty*; she composed her story on scraps of paper which her mother then transcribed.

The story is told from the horse's viewpoint and, as such, broke new literary ground:

> While I was young I lived upon my mother's milk, as I could not eat grass. In the daytime I ran by her side, and at night I lay down close by her. When it was hot we used to stand by the pond in the shade of the trees, and when it was cold we had a nice warm shed near the grove. 'I hope you will grow up gentle and good, and never learn bad ways; do your work with a good will, lift your feet up well when you trot, and never bite or kick even in play.'

> I have never forgotten my mother's advice; I knew she was a wise old horse, and our master thought a great deal of her.

There have been some film and TV adaptations of the story; the first film was an American production in 1921 and the 1972 TV series, *The Adventures of Black Beauty*, is regarded as a classic. It ran to 52 episodes and starred William Lucas, Judi Bowker and Roderick Shaw. It was followed in the early 1990s by *The New Adventures of Black Beauty* which was shot in New Zealand and Australia; again, 52 episode were produced. The stirring theme music to the original series, 'Galloping Home', was part of childhood for many people and can be heard on YouTube now. Sky TV subscription channel aired the 'New Adventures' between 2014 and 2016.

Straight ahead is the market place, selling food such as burgers, sandwiches and fish and chips: there are seats here and it is a pleasant place to have a snack if the weather is fine. Leading off the market are the famous and unique **Yarmouth Rows.** These were once a network of 145 rows so narrow that a special troll cart was designed to carry goods up and down. They originally housed both wealthy merchants and the poor although later becoming the exclusive preserve of the latter, and so the different types of architecture are fascinating. We refer to one famous example, 'Snatchbody Row', when discussing St Nicholas Church above.

Taking a right hand turn down Stonecutters' Way will bring you to Hall Quay with the imposing sight of the River Yare crossing your path.

South Quay and **Hall Quay** lead on from one another and make a very interesting stroll. **Nelson Museum** is dedicated to the victor of the Nile, Copenhagen, St Vincent and Trafalgar, and is on the South Quay. It is good fun for children with sailors' games and a 'swaying deck'.

The **Elizabethan House Museum** is also here. This has a series of rooms showing life at home in the sixteenth century. At 21 South Quay is the **Port and Haven Commissioner's Office**, built in 1909 by Olly and Hayward. It has offices, including a cash office, downstairs, while a Jacobean-style staircase leads up to a boardroom. Some of it is knapped flint and other parts sixteenth-century brick. The Port and Haven Commissioners were appointed in 1670 to keep the Haven and Pier in good repair and they had the authority to levy duties on incoming goods for this purpose. By early Victorian times they were very powerful and had authority separate from the Town Council. Many of their eighteenth- and nineteenth-century papers survive in the Great Yarmouth Borough Archives. On Hall Quay you cannot miss the Town Hall, opened on 31 May 1882 by the Prince of Wales. Like Norwich Thorpe Station of the same period, it was designed to look splendid. Tours are sometimes possible. On the other side of the road you can see and take a tour of the beautiful *Lydia Eva* which is the last surviving steam drifter of the herring fleet. She was used in the Second World War for salvage work but then fell into decline. In 2018, the *Great Yarmouth Mercury* reported that, following boiler and other repairs funded by the Heritage Lottery to the tune

The Port and Haven Commissioner's Office

of £750,000, she had taken to sea once more, and it is hoped that excursions will be possible.

Nearby are the remnants of the thirteenth-century **Greyfriars Cloisters**, now converted into a number of dwellings which you can visit. See English Heritage website for details.

Any left-hand turn will take you eventually, with a few twists and turns, to Yarmouth's famous seafront but the most direct route is at the end of South Quay, down Queens Road which leads directly onto Kings Road and onto Marine Parade. Straight across the road ahead of you is the exquisite **Merrivale Model Village**, with over 200 miniature buildings that kids will love. It has its own street lights that come on when the sun goes down. A few hundred yards to the left is Wellington Pier – there is another, Britannnia Pier, a half-mile further on – and one of the unusual attractions of the town, the **Sea Life Centre**, which has an aquarium with an underwater tunnel. Turn right and walk down South Beach Parade until you reach Nelson's Monument.

Great Yarmouth Town Hall

The Lydia Eva

'I am a Norfolk man, and glory in being so.'

Vice Admiral Horatio Nelson,
addressing a crowd in Great Yarmouth.

Nelson's Monument is, at 144ft high slightly shorter than the other one in Trafalgar Square, London, which stands at 169ft. Nelson reputedly came ashore here several times, one of the most famous being after the Battle of

Copenhagen in 1807 when his first call was the nearby naval hospital (you passed it on the way here) where he spent two hours visiting the wounded sailors. Such concern for his men was unusual at the time and helps explain why he was seen as a hero by them, as well as by his adoring Norfolk public. Folklore has it that on another of his journeys through the town the landlady of the Yarmouth pub 'The Wrestler's Arms' asked him if she could change the name to 'Nelson's Arms' in his honour, but Nelson replied, laughing, to the effect that this might seem strange as he only had one arm.

A poem was written by the Irish poet George Croly about the monument on a stormy night in 1818. It concludes:

And now the Sun sinks deeper, and the clouds,
In folds of purple fire, still heavier lour;
'Till sudden Night the shore and Ocean shrouds;

The Nelson Museum

But thro' the tempest gleams that stately tow'r,
A giant height, on which the Sun-beams show'r
Their undiminish'd glories. NELSON's name
Is on the pillar. — Thus the stormy hour,
The clouds of battle, shew'd his spirit's flame,
Brighter and broader. — Thus shall blaze the Hero's fame.

Walk back again along the seafront, past the Sea Life Centre and seek out a most worthwhile attraction set halfway between Marine Parade and South Quay. Situated in a former curing works on Blackfriars Road, the **Time and Tide Museum** tells the story of the Yarmouth herring industry and was set up using £2.5 million from the Heritage Lottery Fund. Here you can see the Gorleston Hoard, a collection of over thirty objects including copper axe-heads, spearheads and sword fragments found during building works in 1962 and 1966.

Folklore

Rebecca Nurse from Great Yarmouth hanged in the New World at Salem

This tale is undoubtedly true in the main, although some facts often change in the telling.

Rebecca Nurse set sail to America from Great Yarmouth in 1637 along with her parents and five siblings. She was married to Francis Nurse, an Englishman, in 1644 and had eight children, four boys and four girls. On 23 March 1692 she was arrested in Salem, accused of witchcraft and 'possessing' a group of young girls. 'I am as innocent as the child unborn', she is reputed to have said but she was put on trial without a defence lawyer; her younger sisters, Sarah and Mary, were also arrested on similar charges.

It was claimed that the young girls suffered spasms – which they also did while giving evidence in court – and that Rebecca had been 'tormenting' them, and this included her spirit getting into their beds at night.

She was found not guilty, upon which the spasms of the girls increased and the folk of Salem demonstrated. In September 1692 the verdict was revised to 'guilty' and she was sentenced to death. Sir William Phips, the

British Governor, then intervened and once again reversed the decision, sparing her life. However, pressure was brought to bear on him and he reverted the sentence to guilty once more. She was hanged along with her sister, Mary, two months later.

Subsequently the main witnesses for the (uncontested) prosecution relented, claiming that Satan had made them do it, although it may well have been the result of land disputes. Sarah, Rebecca's sister, was given nine gold sovereigns as 'compensation'.[22]

You are now close to the town's shopping centre and a short walk along Tolhouse Street brings you to the **Tolhouse Museum** which houses a twelfth-century gaol. You can see the original cells and there is a free audio guide describing the experiences of prisoners. It is next to the library where there are toilet facilities.

The walk ends here leaving you close to the centre of town.

The Tolhouse Museum

Finds of both fossils and historical artefacts sometimes occur after storms and have been found in Great Yarmouth. The following relates to an event in the northern part of town. Francis Worship writes in *Norfolk Archaeology* of how, following,

> the awful hurricane on Tuesday, 28th February 1860 ... a man engaged in collecting boulders for building purposes, found on a sand-hill on the North Denes a decayed leathern bag containing seventy silver groats of Henry VIII ... The silver is of inferior quality, and all the coins appear to be of 'the very bad money'... issued in the 36th and 37th years of Henry's reign.

Three miles west of Great Yarmouth, at the west end of Breydon Water, lies the village of **Burgh Castle**, site of a very impressive Roman fort with three of its four walls relatively intact. Numbers 3 and 7 buses go near enough to allow the rest of the trip to be made on foot. The site is open to the public and there is a free car park but this closes at 6.00 pm. The site was built in about the third-century AD and possibly occupied until the fifth century. It served as part of the Roman coastal defences. Controversially, it has been suggested that, from AD 630 it may have been an Irish monastery founded by Saint Fursey. In the eleventh century the Normans erected a

View of the River Yare from Burgh Castle

motte here and used the Roman fort as a bailey. There is a church nearby, **St Peter and St Paul**, the walls of which contain brick and stonework from the fort.

For walkers, the **Angles Way** from Great Yarmouth leads to the site and is a fabulous walk of about four miles (it carries on to Thetford).

Roman remains have been found in this area for many hundreds of years. Sir Thomas Browne, in his *Hydriotaphia* of 1658, says that the most frequent discovery of urns and coins in Norfolk 'is made at the two Caistors by Norwich and Yarmouth, at Burgh Castle and Brancaster.'

About three miles away, in Beccles Road, **St Olaves** (if coming by foot there is a path leading from the A143), is the complete undercroft of a small Augustinian Priory founded by Roger FitzOsbert and dedicated to Olaf, Christian King of Norway who it is said offered his subjects 'baptism or death'. After falling into disrepair the building became a private house until 1902. Further details on English Heritage website.

Notes and contact details

Norfolk Motorcycle Museum, www.mc-museum.freeserve.co.uk
    Check times of opening as they vary.
Happisburgh Lighthouse, www.happisburgh.org/lighthouse
Horsey Windpump and Mere, www.nationaltrust.org.uk
    Tel: 01263 740241. Open March to October; times vary.
Stow Mill, www.stowmill.co.uk Tel: 01263 720298
Waxham Great Barn. Tel: 01692 598824
Caister Castle and Motor Museum. www.caistercastle.co.uk
    Tel: 01664 567707 Open May to September but not on Saturdays.
    There is a café and disabled facilities.
South East Tower, www.greatyarmouthpreservationtrust.org
    Tel: 01493 859640
Nelson Museum, www.nelson-museum.co.uk Tel: 01493 850698
Time and Tide Museum, www.museums.norfolk.gov.uk
    Tel 01493 743930. Admission prices can vary so best check
    in advance. A person with disabilities can bring in another free
    of charge. A ticket lasts all day so you can nip in and out.

Elizabethan House Museum, 4 South Quay. www.museums.norfolk.
gov.uk Tel: 01493 745526. Open April to October at various times.

Great Yarmouth Town Hall, www.great-yarmouth.gov.uk
Tel: 01493 846125

The Lydia Eva, www.lydiaeva.org.uk

The Tolhouse Gaol, www.museums.norfolk.gov.uk 01493 858900

Sea Life Centre, www.sealife.co.uk Tel: 01493 330631. Check in
advance for admission times and prices

Merrivale Model Village, www.greatyarmouthmodelvillage.co.uk
Tel: 01493 842097 Open in the summer months; various admission
prices.

Burgh Castle fort and St Olave's Priory, www.english-heritage.org.uk
Tel 0370 3331181

CHAPTER 3

Central Norfolk

Central Norfolk – west: heading south from King's Lynn

'This is Norfolk', he said to himself; and in that intense, indrawn silence some old atavistic affiliation with fen-ditches and fen-water and fen-peat tugged at his soul and pulled it earthward.

A Glastonbury Romance by John Cowper Powys,
published in 1932, written in New York and set in the Fens.

Millennia ago, the land to the south of King's Lynn, and hugging the Wash, now called the Fens, was oak forest which then became flooded and consequently a massive bog. The Romans had a go at drainage but it was only 200 years ago that a really successful scheme was tried, with the result that fabulously rich peat soils were produced and this has been intensively cultivated ever since. The Fens have been called Britain's largest man-made landscape and a flat place of parallel lines – with the occasional church or other building which seem out of scale on a horizon that never appears to come any closer as you walk. Looking down, you may occasionally spot the remains of the oaks, in hues of dark ochre, red and blue, colours caused by the minerals absorbed in the wood over time.

Three miles south of King's Lynn on the A47 is **Middleton Mount**, a motte and bailey castle. It is probably the same age as the larger castle at Denton. There is a mound left now which is in the care of Norfolk Archaeological Trust and is open to the public.

There are several churches of great interest in the area. One, **St Mary the Virgin** at **Wiggenhall St Germans** has fine wooden fittings, notably benches dating from the fifteenth century which have carvings in the form of animals and poppyheads (nothing to do with poppies but derived from the Latin word 'puppis', which means 'poop' as in the figurehead of a ship – often they are of the seven deadly sins). It also has a brass in the floor of the south aisle in the shape of a heart and dedicated to Sir Robert Kervile; Sir Robert died abroad and his wife retrieved his heart for burial in the church. In 2018 the *Eastern Daily Press* reported on the strange behaviour of the Victorian organ which, it is claimed, sometimes plays itself – apparently workmen fled in terror when this occurred. Often, supposedly haunted places feel very cold but this church can become hot for no reason.

Downham Market is the market town serving this corner of Norfolk – it has a cast-iron clock tower in the main square which was made in 1878 by William Cunliffe at a cost of £450.

The name 'Downham' means 'settlement on a hill', a feature which would have both protected it from flooding (which was common before effective drainage became possible) and been a defensive feature when it was first formed about 2,000 years ago. A walk around will reveal many buildings constructed of the local carrstone, a fact which caused some to call it 'the gingerbread town' at one time.

It was granted a market charter in 1050 AD and the market became very prosperous under the jurisdiction of Ramsey Abbey. It was famous for trading in horses and especially butter – at one time large quantities of butter were shipped to London via Cambridge whence it picked up the name 'Cambridge Butter'.

It is believed that King Charles I hid in a building standing where the Swan Inn is now on May Day 1646 following the Battle of Naseby – he was disguised as a clergyman. More details about the town's history can be obtained at Downham Heritage Centre which is in Priory Road.

Running through the town is the **Fen Rivers Way**, a fifty mile walking path between King's Lynn and Cambridge.

Some small villages in Norfolk are extraordinarily interesting and **Denver**, just south of Downham Market, is one of them. Take a look at **Denver Sluice**, now home to West Norfolk Rowing Club, and it is still possible to imagine the efforts of Cornelius Vermuyden,who built the first sluice across the river in 1651 to help with drainage of the area. Alas, it burst and had to be replaced in 1713. Denver also has a fully functional windmill, situated on the **Fen Causeway,** a twenty-four-mile path leading from Denver to Peterborough.

Downham Market Clock

   Denver's most famous son is George William Manby (1765-1854), a most eccentric and brilliant man born in 1765. After leaving his wife in 1801, having been shot by her lover, he wrote several learned books and invented many things including the Manby Mortar, which saved perhaps 1,000 men from shipwrecks in his lifetime; an 'unsinkable' ship, the trial for it being possibly sabotaged by sailors who allegedly caused the ship to rock until it turned over (he was not a popular man); a new type of harpoon the demonstration of which was probably again ruined by the ship's crew, and the first pressurised fire extinguisher.

He was an influential man, a member of the Norfolk and Norwich Archaeological Society and not without means; in 1852 he arranged, and paid for, a lithograph to be provided for publication by the society of his birthplace, East Hall in Denver. In a letter about the lithograph, the Reverend George Henry Dashwood FSA describes East Hall as 'a curious relic, as it appears to me, of Tudor domestic architecture'. In later years George Manby

George William Manby, 1818

turned his house into a museum about Nelson. It was an unappreciated life in some ways and his memorial in the village church of All Saints in Hilgay, just down the road from Denver, bears the doleful words: 'The public should have paid this tribute.'

Stow Bardolph, a short walk or drive north of Downham Market, has two attractions of a somewhat different kind. Firstly, the **Church Farm Rare Breeds Centre** is great for kids and has horses, sheep, goats, pigs, donkeys, poultry, guinea pigs and rabbits; there is also a café and shop. Then there is the life-like wax effigy of Sarah Hare in a mahogany cupboard in the Holy Trinity Church. Sarah died in 1744 and left money and instructions for making a life-size effigy of herself, dressed in one of her own gowns with 'a piece of crimson satin thrown in a garment like a picture hair upon my head' (her own written words): it was not to flatter, but to portray her, blemishes and all, for eternity. It has recently been expertly given a new lease of 'life' that should last the next couple of hundred years.

The Welney Wetland Centre, where you can rent binoculars to view rare butterflies, birds, fish and all manner of plants, is nine miles south of Downham Market.

West of Downham Market, on the A1122 lies the village of **Outwell** where a substantial medieval find was made in 2012: a dress fastener, buckle, stud, strap mount, pendant, and a lead cloth seal were discovered by metal detecting.

On the A1122 from Downham Market to Swaffham lies **Marham Castle**, a fortified manor house whose owner, William Belet, was granted the right to crenellate in 1271, although records show that just six years later the 'castle', as it was called, fell foul of the authorities as his work was held to be an 'injurious fortification' and as such, a threat to the king's authority in the area. The house passed into various family members' hands until 1385, when it was held by the abbess and convent of **Marham.**

If **Swaffham** has an air of slightly faded grandeur, this is hardly surprising; its past was very grand, indeed. In the late eighteenth and nineteenth centuries it was no less than a social centre to rival almost anywhere on the Continent. Its fine houses and wide roads welcomed the aristocracy to balls, soirees and concerts; parents would send their sons and daughters here 'for the season', to see and be seen. Lord Orford raced his greyhounds in the Brecks and

The Pentney Hoard found in 1977 by an East Dereham gravedigger at St Mary Magdalene in Pentney (located about eight miles southeast of King's Lynn) contained six silver Saxon brooches. They are now on display in the British Museum

The Butter Cross in the centre of Swaffham was built in 1783 by the Earl of Orford

founded the sport when, in 1776, he offered a prize of 50 guineas to the champion dog in a series of trials lasting four days. Horse racing was very popular, too, but could not compete with this kind of prize money.

Swaffham was named after the Swabian Rhineland immigrants who originally settled here. A Benedictine priory for women was established in the town around the middle of the twelfth century. Another famous establishment was Hammonds Grammar School. One of the boys attending in the 1960s was Harry Carter, the painter responsible for some of Norfolk's most beautiful village signs. His distant cousin was Howard Carter, the famous archaeologist who first entered the tomb of Tutankhamun. He is reputed to have died from the curse of the Pharaohs in 1939 but in reality it was cancer. He is buried in London and his grave has the inscription:

May your spirit live,
May you spend millions of years,
You who love Thebes,
Sitting with your face to the north wind,
Your eyes beholding happiness.

Folklore

The legend of John Chapman

The story goes that a peddler, John Chapman, dreamed that if he could find his way to London Bridge, something wonderful would be told to him. He went to London and stood on London Bridge when a man came up to him and asked him what he was doing there. John Chapman said he was obeying a dream. The other man scoffed and said how foolish it was to believe in dreams, 'for, if I was to stoop as low as thee, I would believe a dream I have just had in which I was told that a man called John Chapman from a town called Swaffham in Norfolk had a tree in his garden under which is a pot of money. Fooey! Thou art a silly old fool!' John Chapman rushed back to Swaffham and dug under the tree in his garden. Lo! There was a box but it was empty. On the lid was a Latin inscription which he posted in his front window, not knowing any classical language. Soon enough, a scholar came by and translated it: 'Under me doth lie another much richer than I'. He dug again and discovered a great treasure. To show his gratitude to God, he paid for the building of the church of St Peter and St Paul in its entirety.

Not far from the statue of Ceres, Roman goddess of the harvest which adorns the market cross, there is the tiny **Swaffham Museum** and Tourist Information Centre combined. It is at 4, London Street and has some Stone Age, Roman and Saxon artefacts and a special section on the discovery of Tutankhamun's tomb by Howard Carter.

An oval jewelled brooch (fibula) of gilt metal set with an amethyst, most probably Roman, was found near Swaffham in 1855. Oval brooches from this period are very rare, one other previously having been found in Suffolk in 1788.

The **church of St Peter and St Paul** is striking – built in 1454 on the site of an earlier church, it is constructed of limestone from Barnack in Northamptonshire. John Chapman, the 'Pedlar of Swaffham' and his dog (story above) are commemorated in the carvings on some of the pew ends.

Swaffham is a good spot to either drop off from or join the Peddars Way which runs about a mile from the town.

The beautifully decorated early sixteenth century tower of St Peter and St Paul in Swaffham

Just north of the town lies **Castle Acre Priory**, one of the most important and largest monastic sites in England. It was founded in 1190 and was the home of the Cluniac order. The west end gable, prior's lodging and substantial remains can be seen along with a garden growing some of the herbs that the monks would have used for medicinal purposes. There would have been up to thirty-six monks here at any time, supported by many servants; this was not an order that believed in hard physical labour, but in contributing to God in more refined ways, such as copying sacred texts. The deed of surrender to Henry VIII upon the suppression of the monasteries was made by the prior, Thomas Malling, and ten monks on 22 November 1537.

In 1853 a report on the Cluniac order was privately published by the Rev. J.H. Bloom, vicar of Castle Acre and Chaplain in Ordinary to His Royal Highness the Duke of Sussex. He gives the itinerary for daily worship:

Matins	3 am
Prime	6 am
Tierce	9 am
Sext	Noon
Nones	2 pm
Vespers	4 pm
Compline or Second Vespers	7 pm

The Cluniac order liked fine food but it could sometimes leave much to be desired. A monk, Guy de Provins, is quoted in the above account:

> When you wish to eat, they make you fast. The night is spent praying in the church; the day in working; and there is no repose but in the refectory; – and what is to be found here? Rotten eggs, beans with all their pods on, and liquor fit for oxen; for the wine is so poor that one might drink it for a month without intoxication.

Also in the village is **Castle Acre Castle**, founded by William de Warenne after the Battle of Hastings, and **Bailey Gate** which is one of two stone gatehouses added about 1200. The castle has a chequered history, being sold several times after the medieval period, and later rebuilding alternated with periods when stone was stripped for road building and other purposes. The castle was placed into state guardianship by the 5th Earl of Leicester in 1971.

Heading south along Cley Road, you pass the Golf Club and then come to **Cockley Cley**, an Iron Age settlement, which has a reconstruction of an Iceni Village and a nature trail. A short drive later along the same road brings you to **Gooderstone Water Gardens**, a 6 acre water garden which has a nature trail over thirteen wooden bridges. Nearby is **Oxburgh Hall**, a moated manor built in 1482 by the Bedingfield family, who still own it.

Castle Acre Bailey Gate

There is a priest hole, hidden doors, an embroidery worked on by Mary, Queen of Scots, and outside, 70 acres of garden to explore.

Early in 1846 in the village of **Beachamwell**, to the north of Oxburgh Hall, a worker was sent to fetch some sand and, in digging about 2 ft below the surface, his spade struck and broke an earthen pot out of which spilled fifty silver coins. The reverses were of Domitian, Vespasian, Nerva, Trajan, Hadrian, Antoninus Pius, Faustina the Elder, Marcus Aurelius, Faustina the Younger, Commodus and Lucius Verus. Why were the coins there? As elsewhere, it is possible that retreating Romans left them; another theory is that burying a pot of coins such as this is an attempt to take possession of the ground, in a manner of speaking.

Beachamwell is also famous for the medieval carving in St Mary's Church of what is known as 'the Beachamwell Devil' – a grinning head with horns and tongue hanging out.

Rejoining the A1065 will lead you to the **Brecks**. The word 'Brecks' means 'a sandy heathland' and once, as the only animal that could thrive here, rabbits were bred in huge quantities guarded over by the, often dreaded, warreners who existed to ensure that the locals could not profit from rabbit meat or fur. **Thetford Warren Lodge**, the highly fortified home of these men, can still be seen. Pingo lakes abound in this area – these were formed when domes of soil covering a core of ice collapsed. Folklore has it that the devil can be summoned by walking three times round a pingo at midnight. The eerie nature of the landscape is enhanced by many twisted Scots Pine trees. In 1914 the government began a huge tree-planting programme over 47,000 acres, which has resulted in the largest lowland pine forest in the country. Roe deer, muntjac and hares can be seen as well as the rabbits nowadays.

Weeting village and St Mary's Church are just off the A1065 just short of Brandon, parking is usually available, and it is possible from here to take

A pingo, located on the Peddars Way, near Knettishall Heath

an interesting walk of about 4½ miles to **Grimes Graves**; the terrain is flat and easy underfoot. Part of the walk is through Thetford Forest with trees of oak, lime and hazel that thrive in the sandy soil hereabouts. We have placed these three interesting places together to form a memorable trip but, if you wish to solely visit Grimes Graves, head out on the A134 where, about 7½ miles north-west of Thetford, there is a car park with free parking for about fifty cars.

Weeting Castle, the remains of which can be seen, was built in the 1130s by Hugh de Plais, a follower of William de Warenne, on the site of a former Anglo-Saxon settlement. It had two storeys: the bottom an undercroft and the upper-floor containing living quarters. In the thirteenth century a large kitchen and a moat were added, the walls being strengthened at the same time with the addition of an external layer of flint. It is considered a fine example of a high-status twelfth-century manor house. The castle was abandoned from the fourteenth century. Some remains, including that of the Hall and chamber block, can be seen today. It is open to the public and managed by English Heritage.

St Mary's Church has a circular tower containing two bells and is also faced with flint. Neglected for centuries after 1400, it was completely restored in the 1900s by John Angerstein, the owner of Weeting Hall (demolished in the 1950s). Seven members of the Angerstein family are buried in a vault here. There are 'clues' to several historical figures in the church: Sir John Howard may have been married here to the daughter of Sir John Plais in the reign of Richard II. The great east window, installed in 1900, was restored and rededicated to Anthony, Bishop of Ely, in 2005.

Folklore

Babes in the Wood

Location: Wayland Wood, Near Watton

This is actually quite a complicated fairy tale centering on the relationships in the de Grey family of nearby Griston Hall between 1541 and 1572. It also involves the Heydons of Baconsthorpe. However, at its core is the story of an evil uncle who paid henchmen to murder his young nephew and niece in order to inherit the family fortune. The paid assassins took the young children to Wayland Wood – often subsequently referred to as Wailing Wood – but losing their nerve, left the babes to starve instead of killing them. The children, unable to look after themselves, died holding hands and a robin covered their bodies with leaves.

The tale was turned into a pantomime in 1827 called *Harlequin and Cock Robin* and it is still performed sometimes, especially in Norfolk. Walt Disney produced a film version which included a community of elves who saved the children. They feature today on the village sign.

There is also a poem, author unknown, which reads:

Thus wandered these poor innocents,
Till death did end their grief,
In one another's arms they dyed,
As wanting due relief:
No burial this pretty pair
Of any man receives
Till Robin-red breast piously
Did cover them with leaves.

Flint mining at **Grimes Graves** dates back to about 3000 BC. The name possibly derives from the belief of the Anglo-Saxons that the pocked landscape – left after mining, described below – was the work of the earth-god Grim, hence 'Grim's Graves'. In the Stone Age flint was needed for tools, especially axes, and thereafter for building work. The Bronze Age saw more sophisticated methods used for making implements of all kinds and the mines at Grimes Graves were largely abandoned. However, flint continued to be in demand and, as late as the Battle of Waterloo in 1815, the area of Brandon generally produced hundreds of thousands of flints for the use of the Duke of Wellington's muskets.

The abandoned Babes in the Wood – illustration by Randolph Caldecott, 1879

It is possible that Grimes Graves also had a religious significance some 5,000 years ago although some of the 'evidence' of fertility rites has been called an elaborate hoax and research is ongoing.

We do know for sure that flint mining was carried out extensively from around 2300 BC and, during the next 500 years, some 400 pits were dug over about 50 acres. Deer farms were established in the area to equip workers

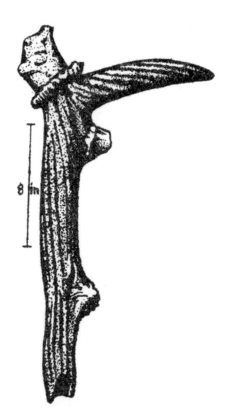

Deer antler picks were used to extract flint

with their mining and hacking tool of choice – antlers; the amount required obviously being great as they did not last long. Thousands of broken antlers have been excavated and can be seen.

As regards mining, probably one new shaft would be dug each year by a team of twelve workers who scooped out the chalk to a depth of about 30 ft until a vein of flint could be found; ladders would be made as they descended. Lateral galleries, about 4 ft high, would then be hacked into the flint. The lowest recorded was 2 ft high and the longest 25 yards. The flint would be sent to the open ground by basket and rope. Up to 8 tons were mined in this way, whereupon either the vein became exhausted or the rains came and flooded the mine. In the winter, when mining was impossible, axe-heads and other tools would be fashioned. It is a mystery why so many axe-heads were made and simply stored, never to be used. Also, the fact that each year the mine that had previously been worked was filled in with greater care than we might think needful, lends extra credence to the belief that there was some religious aspect to the whole process, or at least that care was taken to not offend the earth-gods unnecessarily. The site certainly does have an unworldly pocked appearance.

Grimes Graves is open from the beginning of March to the end of October and is free to members of English Heritage. It is possible to descend one of the deeper mineshafts and view the lateral galleries.

In some parts of Thetford Forest Park close to Grimes Graves, such as **Harling**, substantial Roman and medieval finds have been made by people field-walking – notably pottery and metal objects including buckles.

From Grimes Graves it is a short distance to **Thetford** (for the most direct route, connect to the A134 which runs close by). Follow signs to the Thetford Priory, the ruins of which are magnificent. This was the Priory of our Lady of Thetford, one of the foremost monasteries in East Anglia and very powerful. It was started in the early eleventh century and for 400 years was the burial place of the Dukes of Norfolk. We have an interesting account of its inception:

> Roger Bigod, the founder, instead of making a pilgrimage to the Holy Land, as he had intended, at the earnest desire of his friends brought some Cluniac monks from Lewes Priory, and established them in a monastery he had commenced in 1104, on the site of the present free school ... The foundation was laid in 1107; and in 1114, the Prior and twelve monks entered and occupied the building, the church having been dedicated to the Blessed Virgin and St Andrew ... Eight days after the foundation was laid Roger Bigod died, and his body was forcibly taken to and buried in Norwich Cathedral by Bishop Herbert; although his earnest desire was to be buried in this Priory-Church... the works were but little retarded; and in seven years was constructed one of the largest monasteries in Norfolk – inferior to Norwich and Walsingham, but superior in extent to Castleacre...[23]

The priory surrendered to Henry VIII in 1540.

Just over a mile distant is the **Church of the Holy Sepulchre**, once neglected and used as a barn but now protected by English Heritage; 1.7 miles away is **Thetford Warren Lodge**, referred to above – the walls at ground level are over a metre thick because attack was always possible from the local population. Before you travel on, **Castle Hill** to the south-east of the town centre is well worth seeing; it is a Norman motte and although no traces of the castle remain it gives wonderful views of the town and surrounding countryside.

Thetford itself is a good place to rest and eat – there are cafés and takeaways. It is famous today as the setting for many of the scenes from the

Thetford Castle Hill

much-loved sitcom Dad's Army – if you wish, you can eat your sandwiches on a bench alongside a seated bronzed statue of Captain Mainwaring. Fans of the series can also see Jones' van, and various steam-powered devices, in the **Charles Burrell Museum**, a short walk away.

A must-see is the **Ancient House Museum** in White Hart Street. As far as can be told, there being no records, it started life as a wealthy merchant's house in the early 1500s. In 1921, the Mayor of Thetford consulted Prince Frederick Duleep Singh[24] about the possibility of setting up a museum in the house which the prince bought and presented to the town. It is now run by the Norfolk Museums Service. The house is an evocative recreation of life in times past – the hall is as it might have been in 1595 and the kitchen has all the latest implements from 1901. It also houses Thetford exhibits.

Folklore

Sasquatch

Location: off A1075 from Dereham to Thetford at various places, notably the forest around Thetford.

There have been sightings since the 1970s of a hairy creature, maybe 7–10 ft tall, which walks sometimes on all fours and sometimes upright. It is reputed to live in the forest and, unusually, does not seem to mind being seen – one man driving his car was able to drive back again, twice, to take a better look and the sasquatch, as it appeared to be, stood tall and stared back at him.

About 14½ miles north of Thetford, on the Peddars Way, lies the site of a Roman military camp, **Saham Toney**. It is about 250 by 200 yards and Celtic horse brasses and other finds with cavalry connections have been uncovered – thus it was almost certainly a Roman marching camp.

Between Thetford and Diss, off the A1066, is Knettishall Heath, and this is where one of the great UK walking experiences starts, The Peddars Way and Norfolk Coast Path.

Walk 6: A Walk along the Peddars Way and Norfolk Coast Path

Distance: 46 miles to Holme, then 83 miles along the coast path to Hopton-on-Sea.

Time to allow: Some people walk the entire path in a matter of days, but most take at least a couple of weeks. There are good, and reasonably priced B&Bs en route and a service for forwarding luggage as you progress. Some parts can be cycled and others ridden on horseback.

Walking Conditions: Knettishall Heath to Holme is very easy-going and flat. The coastal section could hardy be more different – wild, windy and magnificent with some soft, sandy or stony sections which can be hard on the legs. If you can manage, the views gained are unsurpassed and make up for any aches and pains. Detailed information on each section is invaluable

Peddars Way signpost near Castle Acre

prior to venturing out. The authors have written a book on this topic and details are given below.

How did the Peddars Way come about?

This is a great mystery and there are all sorts of theories from serious to crackpot. Some say that the route was formed just after Queen Boudica's very-nearly-successful attempt to drive the Roman invaders into the sea. The theory is that the Emperor Nero ordered the path to be built in order to move his troops quickly over the area and inflict vengeance on the troublesome East Angles, which by all accounts the Romans did with terrible ferocity.

Others say that the route was part of a much longer pathway extending to Cornwall, but the purpose of this has never been satisfactorily explained.

The most intriguing claim is made by those who point out the incredibly straight nature of the path – they pose the very relevant question: 'Who would have wanted to take a super-fast route to Holme? Why?' The solution, say these folk, is to be found in the fact that 500 million years ago Norfolk formed part of what is known as the 'Avalonian Block', which means that it was connected to Europe. Thus the route was a fast track for traders to get to markets on the Continent.

PART 1 Knettishall Heath to Holme: total distance 46 miles

This first part is best considered in manageable chunks; of course, what you consider the right length of each will depend very much on how fit you are and also on how fast you wish to proceed. On our journey, we split it into four, the longest being the first at 14.5 miles; the second, from Little Cressingham to Castle Acre is 11.7 miles; the third, to Sedgeford, is 13.9 miles, and the last, to Holme and Hunstanton, around 8.9 miles. It is marvellous in that, although brimming with interest both on and just off the path, all of it is pretty much accessible to all ages and abilities. You can also cycle most of it and horse riders will find few problems, although they may have sometimes to take a special parallel route.

Here are some features of special interest found as you go along.

Walking the Peddars Way

The first section is very easy and popular with many folk for a walk prior to Sunday lunch. You will cross streams, walk beside dark, tilled fields edged by magnificent trees (the Jay is responsible for many of these as each bird will 'hide' several thousand acorns each spring to theoretically retrieve in the winter) and you may be lucky enough to spot a Red, Roe or Muntjac deer. The Woodlark, Stone Curlew, Woodland Jays, Sparrowhawks and Crossbills are a few of the birds who have taken a liking to the relatively newly planted Corsican pines.

Knettishall Heath

The land has always had precious little commercial value. Once wild horses were to be found here and the Normans introduced rabbits, protected by special 'warreners', referred to above; the rabbit industry was one of the mainstays of employment here right up to the 1930s. Thereafter, the UK government decided to plant hundreds of thousands of pine trees which, even now, you can witness struggling to gain the life-giving sun by straggling upwards often to a great height. Thus was produced the largest manmade forest in England.

You will edge the **Stanford Battle Area**, which is a training area for the British Army. In 1942 the government decide to evacuate the villages of Buckenham Tofts, Langford, Stanford, Sturston, Tottington and West Tofts, assuring the villagers that their homes would be available again after the war. Unfortunately, this was not the case, and the area remains a training ground for UK troops going to Afghanistan and elsewhere. There is a tragic and legendary story of Lucilla, a resident who began a fruitless five-year campaign to regain her home. In 1950 she was told she would never be allowed to return and on Remembrance Day, she hanged herself.

This is pingo country and you will see some of these small ponds which, 20,000 years ago, were hills of ice.

Just off the path is **Grimes Graves**, the flint mining complex discussed above.

You will pass through some exquisite villages including Little and Greater Cressingham and Castle Acre, where the Cluniac Order became established just after the Conquest. You will also edge **Houghton Hall**, a fine Palladian house, once the home of Sir Robert Walpole, Britain's first prime minister. There used to be a Houghton village – it is in the Domesday Book – but it was probably removed to make way for the Hall; it may well have been almost deserted at the time anyway, and it joins the other 200 'lost' or 'deserted' villages in Norfolk.

Before long the air changes to the salty tang of the immense ocean ahead and so you can both smell and see **Holme-next-the-Sea** before you. The dunes are a wonderland of huge flat golden sands, wild grasses, fungi, moths – this is the 'moth capital of England' as up to 900 different varieties are blown over from the continent – butterflies and dragonflies. A sign near the dunes tells you that you have completed the first section of the journey – the Peddars Way itself.

PART 2 The Norfolk Coast Path – Hunstanton to Hopton-on-Sea: total distance 83 miles

This part of the walk could hardly be more different. It is undoubtedly more challenging and here it is divided it up into seven shorter sections, ranging from about 5 to 9 miles. You cannot take horses here nor bicycles, although there is a special cycleway just a little inland.

Beginning at **Hunstanton** (or Sunny Hunny to the locals), a complete new town built by Henry Le Strange in mid-Victorian times and, before that, the landing place of St Edmund, the first Patron Saint of England, you retrace your steps past Holme and on to Thornham. Here you will see a land of rolling mists and the Thornham stumps.

The path continues past **Brancaster** which, apart from being incredibly beautiful, is legendary in being the spot where Norfolk's greatest sea hero, Admiral Lord Nelson, gained his love of the ocean. We took a breather in **Burnham Deepdale** as it is a good stopping-off point with a campsite, information centre, shops and cafés. The panorama is simply stunning.

From here it is about 8.1 miles to Holkham, along one of Norfolk's most beautiful stretches of coastline. You may get blown about a little! You may like to visit **Holkham Estate**, home of the famous Thomas Coke whose ancestor, the 1st Earl of Leicester, built a beautiful house and began the task of reclaiming this hitherto barren land for agriculture. Details are given in Chapter 2.

For many, the next stage of the walk – about 7.2 miles to **Stiffkey** – is paradise and passes through Wells-next-the-Sea with its endless sandy beaches. It is also a site of international importance, as is much of this coast walk, for rare birds; autumn will see tens of thousands of Pink Geese crossing the skies in a V-shape formation as they begin their migratory odyssey.

You may well spare a thought for the Rector of Stiffkey, Howard Davidson, as you pass by. He was, by all accounts, a fine priest and received his appointment before the Great War, during which he served in the Royal Navy. Coming home after four years was not so happy as he found his wife pregnant; however, he accepted the new daughter as his own

Flock of Pink Geese at Wells-next-the-Sea

and carried on working very hard. In time, he fell foul of some powerful local people due to his habit of travelling to Soho in London and helping the prostitutes there. A private investigator was hired who approached forty girls in London, only one of whom had anything detrimental to say about him and this was when she had been drinking – when sober she tried to recant and attempted suicide. In 1932 Davidson was found guilty by the church authorities of immorality and defrocked. Ever the showman and determined to proclaim his innocence to maximum effect, he took to appearing in a fairground at Blackpool. He would enter the cage of a lion and lioness and talk to the ticket holders. Unfortunately, in the performance on 28 July 1937, he stood on the tail of the lioness and was attacked by the lion. He died two days later and his last words are reputed to have been: 'Did I make the Front Page?' There was great grief at his funeral and people talk of him to this day, most considering him quite innocent of the charges laid against him.

The walk continues to **Cley**, to **Weybourne** and Cromer. You will pass through **Salthouse**, once very prosperous as salt was a most valuable commodity in days gone by. It was also the home of one Onesiphorous Randall, who built a lovely house on the beach. He put a cannon in front of his domain to stop prying eyes as often a carriage could be seen whisking

The beach at Cley

along the sands carrying a beautiful lady. The 'folly', as it was known, lasted until 1953 when it was duly carried away by the sea.

You will pass through **East and West Runton, Sheringham** and into **Cromer**, famed for the 'Cromer Crab'. Once this was also the centre of the herring industry, probably the most important industry in Norfolk.

As already remarked, Sir Arthur Conan Doyle based some of his best Sherlock Holmes stories on things he saw and heard about when on one of his motoring trips in the county. He used to play cricket and golf here sometimes – it is fascinating to wonder if Holmes' chief antagonist, the infamous Professor Moriarty, was based on a man of that name whom he would probably have known from Sheringham Golf Club.

Arguably of even greater importance in the development of the area was a journalist named Clement Scott, who was sent here by his paper, the *Daily Telegraph*, to find out why this part of the coast appealed to so many. He came down and immediately fell in love with the area as well as a local miller's daughter, Louie Jermy. The locality is now known as 'Poppyland' and that is down to him. He wrote the following famous verse in the churchyard of

The Coastal Path leads the walker up Beeston Bump, providing marvellous views of Sheringham

Sidestrand church, just a couple of miles from the end of this trail. He was waiting for his love.

In my Garden of Sleep, where red poppies are spread,
I wait with the living alone with the dead!
For a tower in ruins stand guard o'er the deep,

At whose feet are green graves of dear women asleep!
Did they love as I love, when they lived by the sea?
Did they wait as I wait, for the days that may be?
Was it hope or fulfilling that entered each breast,
Ere death gave release, and the poppies gave rest?
Oh! Life of my Life! On the cliffs by the sea,
By graves in the grass, I am waiting for thee!
Sleep! Sleep!
In the Dews of the Deep!
Sleep, my Poppy-land,
Sleep!

It is true that if you wait for the tide to recede in summer, and walk a little out on the sands, you can look back and see the cliffs, the green of the trees, and an arc of glowing red poppies under the wide metallic blue sky with its characteristic Norfolk primrose edge.

From Cromer it is just under 8 miles to **Mundesley** via Overstrand along some clifftops and pleasant woodland. **Happisburgh** (details of Mundesley and Happisburgh: Chapter 2) is another 6 miles and includes some walking over sandy beaches which can be hard on the legs. The poet, William Cowper, said of this section of the coast that there is 'something inexpressibly soothing in the monotonous sound of the breakers'. The next section to **Caister-on-Sea** is about 10.5 miles and offers sightings of wildlife – birds, butterflies, dragon flies, toads and seals. This can truly be called remote Norfolk in some parts as you may find you have a whole beach to yourself and may not see anyone else for miles. The final 10 miles of the walk is past tern colonies (10 per cent of Britain's breeding population is here) and the golden beaches and attractions of **Great Yarmouth** (details: Chapter 2) before ending in **Hopton-on-Sea**. Flint tools from the Stone Age and artefacts from the Bronze Age have been found in this holiday village. It is also home to the first holiday camp in the UK, Potters Resort, which was opened in 1920 and annually in January hosts the World Indoor Bowls Championships: the BBC covers the final week.

Seal on the beach at Horsey. Over 2,000 pups were born on this stretch of coast during the 2018/19 winter season

Central Norfolk – west: heading north from King's Lynn

'Most people have got at least one foot in the water,' said Mrs Barrable, 'and they do say a lot of the babies are born web-footed, like ducks.'

Arthur Ransome, *Coot Club* (1934), the fifth of the *Swallows and Amazon* series where Dick and Dorothea Callum visit Norfolk during the Easter Holidays.

From King's Lynn, it is interesting to head out on the A148 towards Great Massingham; if you have time an alternative is to proceed in the same general direction, but to take the 'B' roads where there are many quintessential Norfolk villages and where you will find some ancient churches, flint and carstone cottages and pleasant pubs. **Great Massingham** itself is noted for the number of its ponds and ducks thereupon, providing unique photographic opportunities for visitors. The pub is, of course, called the

Great Massingham Pond

Dabbling Duck. These ponds may have originally been fishing ponds for an eleventh century Augustinian abbey. Robert Walpole, Britain's first prime minister, went to school here. Sadly, over 600 servicemen stationed at the base – the dilapidated control tower of the airfield can still be seen – died in the last war and some of them are buried at nearby St Andrews Church in Little Massingham.

A few miles distant, in Tatterford, is **Houghton Hall**. A fine example of Palladian architecture, the Hall was built in the 1720s for Robert Walpole. It has interiors by William Kent and is surrounded by parkland where exotic deer roam. Also to see is the famous walled garden, a kitchen garden and a model soldier museum. Sculptures by notable artists are on display in the grounds. In 2018 there was also a display of art by Damien Hirst.

You can 'drop down' from here to visit **Castle Acre,** one of the greatest medieval sites in Norfolk, already discussed in the previous section.

Folklore

The Brown Lady

East Raynham is the location of **Raynham Hall,** built in the seventeenth century but only occasionally open to the public. It gives its name to the five estate villages known as the Raynhams. It is reputed to be home to perhaps the most famous ghost in Norfolk, the 'Brown Lady', so known as she wears a brown satin dress. She was the second wife of Charles Townshend, who locked her away claiming that she had committed adultery with the notorious womaniser and drunkard, Lord Wharton; she died of smallpox in 1726. King George IV claimed that she came and stood by his bedside when he visited the house. Her ghost has also purportedly been seen on several other occasions in the house and some staff are said to have given in their notice as a consequence. What makes the story special, however, is that there exists a photograph of her, taken in 1936 by a reporter, Captain C. Provand, who was working for Country Life magazine – it was published and can be seen on the internet today, so anyone can have an opinion, but as to its authenticity, the jury is still out.

Travelling north, however, from Houghton and Raynham Halls, will soon bring you to the start of **Ringstead Downs,** chalk grassland stretching forty miles to Mundesley.

While in the area, there is a chance to see a working windmill in the village of **Great Bircham** – there were once 300 working mills in Norfolk but today most of those you see are incomplete.

North of Fakenham, off the B1355, lies **Creake Abbey,** the beautiful and peaceful setting belying a tragic history. It was originally founded in 1206 by Sir Robert and Lady Alice de Nerford; in 1225 Henry III elevated its status to an abbey. However, a fire in 1484 resulted in necessary demolition of some parts, and in the early sixteenth century the plague reduced numbers to one – the abbot himself, who reputedly died alone in 1506 whereupon the abbey reverted to the crown. There is a café and shops and a regular farmers' market.

About a mile south of South Creake you can find the field in which **Bloodgate Hill Fort** stood. It was, like Warham Camp, one of six earthwork forts that date back to the Iron Age. This one has been flattened through centuries of ploughing, but it is easy to appreciate the importance of the hilltop location. There are two interpretation panels. Forts such as this may well have been designed to protect the interests of farmers who in many cases became much more productive because of new tools and implements invented at this time. They may also have been used as a gathering point for important meetings and for protection in times of war and probably attack from jealous neighbours. This site has been excavated to reveal no trace of military use. It is run now by Norfolk Heritage and is open to view at any reasonable time.

Just under eight miles away is **Binham Priory** and **Binham Market Cross**. The priory is one of the most impressive monastic sites in Norfolk. It was founded in 1091 by Peter de Valoines and the history is scandal-ridden; one of the priors, from 1317 to 1335, was William de Somerton who sold off many of the priory's valuable items to finance his experiments in alchemy. The number of monks was always small for such a magnificent priory, peaking at fourteen but reduced to only six in 1539 upon its suppression by Henry VIII. The nave of the priory is now the parish church. A guide book is available with more details of the turbulent history.

See Norwich Castle above for news of the Binham hoard being acquired for the museum.

The Market Cross, a fine example of a medieval standing cross, stands where a market took place from the 1100s to the 1950s.

If you wish to make a touring base in this area the market town of **Fakenham** is a good choice. It is just under ten miles south of Binham along the A148. **Pensthorpe Nature Reserve** on the Fakenham Road was home to the BBC's Springwatch programme – the reserve is a vast network of meadows, wetlands, woodlands, and even a bug trail. It is a bird-watcher's paradise. North of the town is the **Slipper Chapel** at Houghton St Giles which was built in the fourteenth century as the last chapel for pilgrims on the way to the Walsingham shrine. Many people, some claim this includes Henry VIII himself, walk the last mile to the shrine in bare feet. The 20 acres of **Walsingham Abbey grounds** containing the ruins of a twelfth-century

Binham Market Cross

abbey await. The Shirehall Museum acts as the gateway and holds artefacts and photographs of the village. **The Shrine of Our Lady of Walsingham** was founded by Lady Richeldis in 1061, suppressed by Henry VIII and restored from 1922. It attracts pilgrims from all over the world today. The image of Our Lady is contained in the Holy House, which is itself in the ornate shrine church. There is a very active body of local people willing to help with pilgrimages, even assisting with accommodation – see below.

The remains of Walsingham Priory, photographed with kind permission of the Walsingham Estate Office. Thousands of beautiful snowdrops can be seen here in early spring

Walsingham Priory was plundered by Henry VIII in 1538. The prior, Richard Vowell, helped in the demolition and in handing over the treasure and so received a pension of £100 a year – a vast sum. 'The Walsingham Lament' was written at the time:

Weepe, weepe, O Walsingham,
Whose dayes are nights,
Blessings turned to blasphemies,
Holy deeds to dispites.
Sinne is where our Lady sate,
Heaven turned is to helle;
Satan sitthe where our Lord did swaye,
Walsingham O farewell!

Not to be missed, if you can, is the **Wells and Walsingham Light Railway** which is the world's longest 10¼in narrow-gauge steam railway and will

The Gatehouse was the original entry to Walsingham Priory and was built circa 1440. Located on the High Street

take you on a gentle 5 mph ride, through the most beautiful countryside, from Walsingham to Wells. It takes about half an hour.

The Fakenham Hoard was discovered here in 2015 consisting of eleven gold staters (a type of gold coin, originally minted in Greece but later in Europe).

In 2019 it was announced that a grant from the EU of £33,500, topped up with £8,000 of local funding, was to be used in setting up the **Fakenham**

The Walsingham Pump House at Common Place was built in the sixteenth century

Heritage Trail linking twenty-nine of the town's top attractions and sites. Each will have a plaque with a QR code for information. Details can be obtained from the library.

Notes and contact details

For details of the Fens and walking trails, churches and other sites of interest, www.visitwestnorfolk.com

Downham Tourist Information Centre. Tel: 01366 383287 There are various very good hotels, eateries and pubs in the area.

Fen Rivers Way, www.countrysideaccess.norfolk.gov.uk

Church Farm Rare Breeds Centre, enquiries@ churchfarmsstowbardolph.co.uk Tel: 01366 382162

The Welney Wetland Centre, www.wwt.org.uk Tel 01353 860711

Swaffham Museum, www.swaffhammuseum.co.uk Tel: 01760 721230

Castle Acre, customer@english-heritage.org.uk Tel: 01760 755394.
There is an audio tour provided by English Heritage and a
guidebook on sale.
Iceni village, www.icenivillage.com Tel: 01760 724588
Gooderstone Water Gardens, www.gooderstonewatergardens.co.uk
Tel: 01603 712913
Oxburgh Hall,www.nationaltrust.org.uk Tel: 01366 328258
Brecks, info@visitnorfolk.co.uk
Grimes Graves, www.english-heritage.org.uk Tel: 01842 810656.
There is a Flint Festival in July run by English Heritage.
Priory of Our Lady of Thetford is managed by Thetford Town Council
and is open all year, although closing earlier in the winter months.
Tel 01842 754038
Ancient House Museum www.museums.norfolk.gov.uk Tel: 01603 493625
Peddars Way information, www.nationaltrail.co.uk The book *Peddars
Way and the Norfolk Coast Path* by Stephen Browning and Daniel
Tink is published by Halsgrove at £14.99 and includes information
on planning, what to take etc.
Houghton Hall, email@houghtonhall.com. Tel: 01485 528569.
At time of writing it has 86 per cent ratings of either 'excellent' or
'very good' on www.tripadvisor.com
Ringstead Downs, www.norfolkwildlifetrust.org.uk Tel: 01603 625540
Great Bircham Windmill, www.birchamwindmill.co.uk
Tel: 01485 578393
Creake Abbey, www.creakeabbey.co.uk
Bloodgate Hill Fort, www.heritage.norfolk.gov.uk
Binham Priory, customer@english-heritage.org.uk Tel: 0370 333 1181
Pensthorpe Nature Reserve, www.pensthorpe.com Tel: 01328 851465
Walsingham Abbey Grounds, www.walsinghamabbey.com
Tel: 01328 820259
Shrine of Our Lady of Walsingham, accom@owl-shrine.org.uk
Tel: 01328 820255
Wells and Walsingham Light Railway, www.wellswalsinghamrailway.
co.uk Tel: 01328 711636

Central Norfolk – east: beginning on the southern border of the county in Diss and heading north. (With some zig-zags, towards the coast; the Norfolk Broads)

Dear Mary,
Yes, it will be bliss
To go with you by train to Diss,
Your walking shoes upon your feet;
We'll meet, my sweet, at Liverpool Street.

> Excerpt from *A Mind's Journey to Diss*, Sir John Betjeman.
> The poem is addressed to Mary Wilson, wife of the
> Labour Prime Minister, who grew up in the town.

Sir John Betjeman found **Diss** to be a most attractive town, centred as it is around a large mere with a park in the south, where waterfowl come to feed. There are interesting buildings dating from Tudor times to the present and a good range of shops including the Diss Publishing Bookshop. According to Francis Blomefield's *Topographical history of the county of Norfolk, etc*, the town was originally called 'Dice' which is an Anglo-Saxon word for a stretch of water.

Diss Museum in The Shambles is tiny and tells the story of the town.

Diss is noted for a Camping – or 'Kamping' – match, which was a kind of medieval football played in East Anglia. The games were played with a bladder

Diss Mere

full of dried peas. Many of the county's warriors and strong men would travel miles to take part in these events, which were usually held on a Sunday or holiday. Rules varied from place to place, but it was commonly stipulated that men should be under 25 and unmarried. Boots would oftentimes be tipped with horn. In the 1700s a Camping match was held between Norfolk and Suffolk. Normally up to twenty-four players took part – this time there were about 300 on each side. The 'ball' was thrown onto the 'pitch' and for a while everyone chased it. Then, however, the ball was lost to sight and a bloody punch-up ensued for fourteen hours; nine men died.

Robert Forby, in his *Vocabulary of East Anglia,* 1830, gives a long account of the game. There were two varieties of it, 'rough-play' and 'civil-play'. In the former, fists could be used; in the latter only kicking and wrestling were allowed. In both versions, the goals were 120 yards apart. Mr Charles Mackie's *Norfolk Annals* mentions a match in Norfolk as late as 1831, but this could have been more akin to our idea of modern rugby, which possibly grew out of the gentler version of the sport.

In 1992 at Hoxne, just a few miles south of Diss, a metal detectorist discovered the largest cache of late Roman gold in the Roman Empire. It is called the Hoxne Hoard and consists of gold, silver and bronze coins and 200 items of silver tableware and gold jewellery. It was discovered as a local farmer had lost his hammer and asked a friend, who had a metal detecting machine, to scan a field for it. It is valued at just under £3 million and is in the British Museum. One theory is that it was buried in a remote spot by a local wealthy family from somewhere in East Anglia, and that they failed to retrieve it.

Folklore

The Mistletoe Bride of Brockdish Hall

Just off the A143 lies Brockdish Hall, six miles east of Diss. The story of the Mistletoe Bride is famous – it was the subject of a macabre Victorian song – and yet the details are contested, with several other Norfolk houses claiming to be the location of the story. The tale maintains that at the wedding of a baron's daughter to Lord Lovell in the 1830s, the young bride became bored with the apparently endless wedding celebrations and proposed a game of hide-and-seek. She ran off to a lonely part of the Hall finding a very old trunk which she thought would make an ideal place to hide, and jumped in. When no one came to discover her she tried to release the three locks which held the lid tight but could not. Her bridegroom and all the wedding guests tried in vain to find her but her cries went unheard as the trunk was made of thick old English oak. 50 years later her body was found clutching a sprig of mistletoe. There is a poem about it:

> They sought her that night and they sought her next day
> and they sought her in vain while a week passed away;
> in the highest, the lowest, the loneliest spot,
> Young Lovell sought wildly, but found her not.
> And years flew by and their grief at last,
> was told as a sorrowful tale long past.

Also, just off the A143 is the remains of a motte and bailey castle at **Denton**. The motte is about 150 ft in diameter with a horseshoe-shaped bailey. Possibly built just after the Norman Conquest by William d'Albini, it was destroyed in 1254 and the site is under the care of the National Trust.

Local villages all have their points of interest. Nearby **Banham** has a famous zoo. There is a great enthusiasm in Norfolk generally for steam engines, especially of the Victorian era and **Bressingham Steam and Gardens** is very popular – it has the 6100 Royal Scott locomotive as well as several narrow-gauge rail tracks. It is also the home of the national Dad's Army exhibition (fans note that nearby Thetford has Captain Mainwaring's statue and Jones' van – see above).

Attleborough is basically a Georgian town with a beautiful church, **St Mary's**, built in Norman and Early English styles. Outside is one of two pyramids in Norfolk: this one is 6 ft high and commemorates local Egyptologist William Henry Brooke who died in 1929. The other is at Blickling Hall and contains the remains of John Hobart, 2nd Earl of Buckinghamshire and his two wives. More recently, in the Great War, Attleborough was famous for having both its football and cricket teams sign up as 'Pals' Units'. **Forncett**

St Peter is home to the Norfolk Tank Museum, open from Easter.

In 2014 a local student from the University of East Anglia, Tom Lucking, was metal detecting six miles north of Diss when he discovered what has become known as the Winfarthing Pendant. It was discovered on the grave of an Anglo-Saxon lady of means dated about AD 650–75. The pendant is gold and inlaid with hundreds of tiny cloisonne-set garnets. *The Eastern Daily Press* announced in 2018 that it had been purchased for the Norfolk Museums Archaeology collection.

Just south of Attleborough on the B1077 is Old Buckenham, where there are the remains of two castles, **Old Buckenham Castle** and **Buckenham Castle**. The first was built by William D'Aubigny after the Conquest and little is left, especially as a priory was built on the remains. The

1884 drawing showing the ground and elevation of Denton Castle

D'Aubigny family built a new castle two miles away in the Anarchy (more details: Chapter 4) and this was a much grander affair. It had an inner and two outer baileys; the circular keep had walls 11 ft thick and it may have been 40 ft tall. It was demolished in 1649, leaving the moat and earthworks. The site is Grade I listed and is privately owned.

In 2018 the *Eastern Daily Press* reported that amateur detectorists had made significant finds in **Old Buckenham** – two Roman brooches, a decorated Anglo-Saxon strap-end and twelve medieval hammered coins of silver. As is the legal requirement, the finds were lodged with the Finds Liaison Officer at Norfolk Historic Environment.

The Quidenham Hoard was discovered in the village of that name in 2014 and this included twenty-two Roman silver denarii and twenty-five Icenian silver pieces. It is possible that they were hidden here by the Iceni. Boudica is buried in the village according to legend.

Iron Age and post-medieval finds have been discovered just east of here in **Carleton Rode**. A little to the north, in **Deopham**, much has been detected including flints from the early Bronze Age, Roman gold and silver coins, as well as early Saxon brooches and vessels; all this points to a major Roman settlement and subsequent long-term occupation.

Of special interest is **Wymondham**. Traditionally, the town grew fairly wealthy on wool and also for producing small objects made of wood – spoons, for instance – which it still does. It has a splendid **Market Cross** which doubles as the tourist information centre.

A medieval ringwork has been identified on the Stanfield Estate which could have been started by the d'Albinis about twenty years after the Norman Conquest. A Great Fire ravaged the town beginning 11 June 1615 and was blamed on residents William and John Flooder, among others. Records show that John Flooder was executed on 2 December of that year for the crime. The most famous citizen was William Kett, whose 'rebellion' is told above.

The Market Cross at Wymondham was built in 1617–8 and replaced an earlier medieval structure which was destroyed by a fire in 1615 – see above

The volunteer-run **Mid-Norfolk Railway** travels the eleven miles to Dereham from here.

Most visitors come to see **Wymondham Abbey**. The official website calls it a place 'of welcome, worship and wonder'. It was started in 1107 as a Benedictine monastery and built from Caen stone, as is Norwich Anglican Cathedral. The twin towers can be seen for many miles; Elizabeth I was one of many benefactors. Abbey records show that the wonderful organ by James Davis cost £687 in 1793 and arrived on a cart. The abbey has a fascinating history especially as it began life as a dependency of the Benedictine monastery at St Albans and disputes between the monks of the two religious institutions were common. A special connection has always existed with the murdered St Thomas Becket. There are many legends and treasures here; enquiries as below.

Wymondham Heritage Museum in The Bridewell closes for the winter but returns each spring with a new theme.

Wymondham Abbey

A rare cross, shaped like the Greek letter tau and probably a talisman against the disease St Anthony's Fire, was discovered by a detectorist in **Wramplingham**, north of Walsham in 2018. It dates from 1450–1550 and has been declared treasure. It was thought that the disease was caused by bewitchment and it became a widespread problem in the fifteenth century. Symptoms include mania, convulsions, skin lesions, eventually gangrene and even death. Today we know the condition as ergot and it is caused by a fungal disease on cereal grasses, especially rye, and some flowers. Monks from the Order of St Anthony were known for nursing those affected and, as they lived in an ergot-free area of France, a cure was common. It is now thought that some women who were tried as witches, including those at Salem as discussed above, exhibited symptoms that correlate to ergot poisoning.

Nearby **Hingham** is notable for being fashionable to such a degree in the eighteenth century that, along with Swaffham, some called it 'Little London'. However, prior to this it lost so many prominent citizens to the Americas, beginning in 1633 on a ship called *Bonaventure*, that it petitioned parliament for help because, according to records at the time, the town 'physically, mentally, socially and spiritually', had moved to "New Hingham" in New England.' Among those who moved five years later was Robert Peck, vicar of St Andrew's Church, and half his flock; also, Samuel Lincoln, ancestor of President Abraham Lincoln.

Travelling towards Norwich on the A11 you will see, after about eight miles as you approach the A47, signs for Caistor St Edmund – which was the site of the Roman town of Venta Icenorum. Here is a very rewarding exercise in imagination as there is not much in the way of physical remains, but an information panel gives instructions on downloading a guided walk onto your mobile phone. You can construct the town in your mind as you walk.

History suggests that when the Romans were most successful at subjugating the local population, it was because they actively involved Britons into their projects, giving the conquered race an interest, an investment perhaps, in their rule. This is illustrated at Venta Icenorum, which was built as a trading centre for the Iceni tribe following the disastrous rebellion by Boudica which had been brought about precisely because of the lack of this policy – indeed, the rebellion had been fuelled largely by the Roman administrators' greed and heavy-handedness.

Venta Icenorum Roman Town, as seen today. The town area (now a field) can be seen in the centre of the picture, below St Edmund's Church. The remains of one side of the boundary walls travel diagonally across the picture

This luxurious town was started in AD 70 and the name means 'marketplace of the Iceni'. It had the desired effect and the Iceni were successfully integrated into Roman Britain after twenty or so years. No walls were initially built as the threat of invasion was insufficient to warrant this until AD 270, when the Saxons began incursions. Instead there were houses, a market place, amphitheatre and Roman baths. An impressive feat of building provided running water which flowed by gravity from the far side of the city and then drained into the adjacent river. Each wall of the town as eventually built was over a kilometre long with a strong gate in the middle. They were 23 ft high and 14 ft thick and soldiers could walk along the top. A massive ditch on the outer side was added, some 80 ft wide with an embankment around 17 ft high. This may have been the Roman centre for governing northern East Anglia.

After the Romans left in AD 410, the Saxons added a church upon converting to Christianity and today this is dedicated to St Edmund, usually portrayed as a just and Christian ruler, more details of whose life, death and legend are given in the section on Hunstanton.

Among thousands of finds on the site are prehistoric, Middle Saxon and medieval finds, including pottery and Roman coins, pots, pins, bracelets, a mirror, a purse, rings, a skillet, shoes, spoons, tiles, needles, pendants and knives, and many other artefacts. In 1857 a very rare Roman mirror, or speculum, was discovered – the silver reflective surface probably kept clear by pounded pumice stone used with a sponge. One interesting and varied find in 1859 comprised a figure of Bacchus in bronze, an iron Roman key, a phallus in bronze, parts of three bronze fibulae (brooches), a large Roman green glass bead, a cock in bronze and a bronze ring.

The origins of Roman place names, including that of 'Venta Icenorum', has exercised scholars' minds over the years. This is an explanation given by an eminent Victorian scholar, Dr Guest, and is quoted in the Archaeological Journal of 1889:

> There seems to have been several of these Gwents in Britain; and the Romans obtained their name for the capital towns by turning Gwent into a feminine substantive and then adding the name of the race which inhabited the particular district, as Yenta Belgarum, Yenta Icenorum, Yenta Silurum, &c.

The article continues,

> If therefore this interpretation be accepted, the true meaning of Yenta Icenorum would be the open land, (the Gwent) of the Iceni, and I venture to think that anyone acquainted with the district of which the site of Norwich forms part, especially that portion lying near Caister would quite understand the applicability of the description, certainly with respect to that line of sweeping upland lying along the valley of the Yare from Harford Bridges onwards.

Dereham, also known as East Dereham, is an interesting town a short distance from Norwich – it is on the A47 and buses go direct and frequently from Norwich Bus Station in Surrey Street. The two-towered **St Nicholas Church** is very beautiful and dates from the thirteenth century, with fourteenth and fifteenth century additions.

Folklore

The legend of St Withburga

In the churchyard of St Nicholas Church is **St Withburga's Holy Well**. Legend has it that Withburga, a princess and abbess, founded a nunnery in Dereham. However, she could only find dried bread for her workers and prayed to the Virgin Mary who sent two does which were tame enough to be milked, and this provided the much-needed sustenance. However, the local overseer did not approve and hunted the does with his dogs; for his sins he was thrown from his horse and killed, an act commemorated on the town sign. Following her death in 743, Withburga's body was initially interred in Ely cathedral but fifty-five years later was transferred – the story says that it was completely undecayed – to her church in Dereham. In 974, Brithnoth, the jealous abbot of Ely envied the money that pilgrims were bringing to Dereham on account of her tomb there and stole the body back, using copious amounts of alcohol to make her protectors drunk and insensible. A spring miraculously arose in her violated tomb and this brings pilgrims to this day; it has never run dry.

This cannibal in three years space three hundred martyrs slew
They were his food, he loved so blood, he sparèd none he knew.
Reference to Bishop Bonner in
Foxe's Book of Martyrs 1563, John Foxe.

The town is also famous for Bishop Bonner, who is immortalised in **Bishop Bonner's Cottage Museum** of local history. Bishop Bonner was vicar of Dereham from 1534 to 1538. He rose to become Bishop of London under Henry VIII. Under Mary, he is said to have been instrumental in sending over 200 persons, including some children, for burning at the stake for the crime of heresy against the Catholic Church. He died in prison in 1569 having fallen foul of Elizabeth I.

The town is also linked to poet William Cowper who settled there in later life. He was bullied as a boy, remarking that he knew the buckles of his tormentor's shoes much better than his face.[25] Suffering all his life from

St Nicholas Church and adjacent Bell Tower

depression, he was so sensitive it is said that when the love of his life, Mary Unwin, died in 1796 she was buried in secret at midnight so as to cause him as little distress as possible. Some of his poetry has entered the everyday such as:

> God moves in a mysterious way,
> His wonders to perform.
> He plants his footsteps in the sea,
> and rides upon the storm.

Another well-known observation is:

> Variety's the very spice of life,
> That gives it all its flavour.

St Withburga's Tomb

Often he is funny, as here:
A fool must now and then be right, by chance.

Coprolite is a term for fossilised dung from ancient creatures, and mining it was an important industry in Norfolk in the nineteenth century. Fossils generally have much of their original matter replaced over time with silicates and calcium carbonates; it was known that, treated with acid or

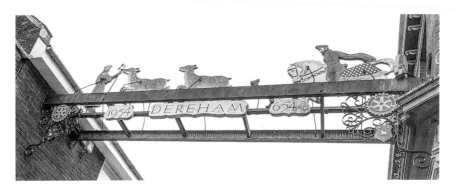

Dereham Town Sign featuring St Withburga

Bishop Bonner's Cottage Museum

water, this material would produce high quantities of phosphates and in 1842 an extraction process was invented and patented by the Rev. John Stevens Henslow which led to industrial scale excavations in the East of England. It was led by the Fisons Company, headquartered in Ipswich which actually still has a Coprolite Street.

In 1873 a rich seam of coprolite – from marine creatures and sharks mainly – was discovered in West Dereham. In Norfolk as a whole, mining was widespread as valuable phosphates nodules also accrued alongside fossils of all types, thus making the surrounding soil valuable.

An acknowledged expert in the area at the time was geologist William Buckland who was so enthusiastic about the product that he reputedly had a pair of coprolite earrings made for his wife.

Billingford is a village about 3½ miles north of Dereham. A Romano-British settlement lies between the River Wensum and Elmham Road. It may have originally been called Billingeford which means 'the ford of Billa's people'. The site, now a Scheduled Ancient Monument, was probably inhabited into the early Anglo-Saxon period and a beautiful gold amulet has been discovered there.

Gressenhall Farm and Workhouse is a famous Norfolk attraction just north of Dereham. Adults and children are well catered for and can learn about rural Norfolk and life in the workhouse. It is presented with flair and imagination with rides, audio features, photography and interpretive panels. Of great interest over recent years in Norfolk has been a 'Voices from the Workhouse' project. Various short videos include 'Ghosts of Gressenhall'. Outside there are beautiful walks. There is a good café and both this and the main attraction fare very well on Tripadvisor.

About equidistant from Dereham and Fakenham on the B1145, a pre-Conquest route which crosses the county east to west, lay **Mileham Castle**; it is possible that the castle was designed to extract tolls from traffic criss-crossing the area. It is large, was built around AD 100 and would have been imposing – it had a motte and two baileys, plus further enclosures with possibly also a deer park. It was abandoned around 1300. The area is also significant for the discovery in 1839 of a square silver dish, the Mileham Dish, now in the British Museum. The dish has been exhibited in France, Tokyo and Japan and, despite intense interest in the area, no other artefacts have been found.

Gressenhall Workhouse Museum, by kind permission of Norfolk Museums Service

Gressenhall Farm, by kind permission of Norfolk Museums Service

Nearby villages include **Swanton Morley**, home of the ancestors of Abraham Lincoln, and **Lenwade** which houses a **Dinosaur Adventure Park**. **Booton** has the extraordinary church, some say folly, of the **church of St Michael and All Angels**, designed by the Reverend Whitwell Elwin, descended from Pocahontas (see Heacham). It is a Gothic fantasy with all the Reverend's favourite bits and pieces from other church designs. With its skinny twin towers, minarets and intricate windows it looks like something from the grounds of Hogwarts. **Beetley**, west of Swanton Morley, is interesting in that in 1991 some rare medieval finds were made here: a medieval copper alloy harness pendant, a late Saxon copper alloy bridle cheek-piece and a ring of the same period. The pendant has red enamel-work and the ring a surface of white metal.

Just north of Beetley on the B1110 is the important historical village of North Elmham. Here you can see the remains of the **North Elmham Chapel** – under the care of English Heritage and free to enter – which, in late Saxon times was the headquarters of the Bishops of East Anglia, before the episcopal seat was moved to Thetford and then Norwich. Excavations suggest a previous wooden building on the site which may have been the

North Elmham village sign

Free parking available for visitors of North Elmham Chapel

Anglo-Saxon Cathedral. Bishop Henry le Despenser, suppressor of the Peasants' Revolt described earlier, used the chapel as a house. It fell into ruin in the late 1600s. Also in the village is the imposing **church of St Mary**, which replaced the cathedral as the place of worship. It is famed for its eight bells and, inside, has some exquisite carving, particularly the medieval pew ends and seventeenth-century pulpit. A medieval wall painting was recently discovered and has been partly restored.

Folklore

The last Norfolk Duel

Location: stone monument in the village of Cawston on the B1145, eleven miles north of Norwich

This stone with an urn on top commemorates the last duel fought in Norfolk on 20 August 1698. It took place on a Saturday morning and the quarrel was between the owner of Blickling Hall, Sir Henry

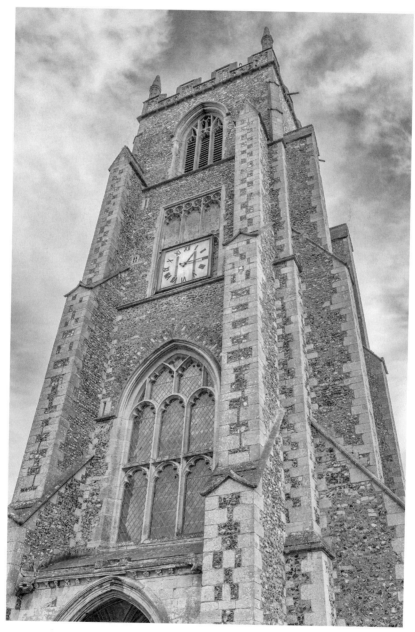

The church of St Mary, North Elmham

Hobart, and Oliver Le Neve of Witchingham Hall. It was a matter of honour as Sir Henry – knighted by Charles II at the tender age of 13 and at the time a renowned swordsman – believed that Le Neve had been spreading rumours about his bravery and loyalty during the 1690 Boyne Campaign. There was only one servant girl present and she hid in the bushes as Sir Henry found his sword caught in Le Neve's clothing enabling his adversary to run him through. Sir Henry died in the south west turret bedroom at Blickling Hall the following day. Apparently unable to accept his defeat to an inferior swordsman, his wailing can sometimes be heard in that part of the house. Le Neve escaped abroad as the duel had been technically illegal, but returned two years later, was put on trial at Thetford Assizes and acquitted.

The countryside and estate surrounding Blickling Hall is beautiful

Blickling Hall, by kind permission of the National Trust

Travelling west beyond Cawston on the B1145 brings you to Aylsham and, just north, to Blickling, the setting for the magical **Blickling Hall**. Originally owned by Sir John Fastolf of Caistor, it passed to Thomas Boleyn, later Earl of Wiltshire, father of Anne Boleyn. Whether she was born here or not is a subject of debate, although an inscription on a painting in the hall says: 'Anne Boleyn born here 1507'. The house as seen today was built on the ruins of the Boleyn property. It passed into the care of the National Trust in 1940.

It is said that no one ever forgets their first view of the magnificent Jacobean redbrick mansion of Blickling. Inside is a wonderful collection of tapestries, plasterwork and furniture, while the library is one of the most

---

Folklore

Anne Boleyn's ghost is said to return to Blickling Hall every 19 May, the anniversary of her execution. It is said that she is driven there by a headless coachman and that she carries her own head under her arm, roaming until daybreak. The local paper, the Eastern Daily Press, has carried some stories in recent years from members of the public who have photographed what are claimed to be paranormal happenings on this night.

significant in England and contains the 'Blickling Homilies'. Outside there is a formal garden and a huge park.

Nearby **Aylsham** is a classic Norfolk market town, with the market being owned by the National Trust. It is also a Cittaslow town – 'Cittaslow' is a movement started in Italy which aims to improve life experience by slowing things down, from traffic to cooking – but perhaps most tourists come to take a ride on the **Bure Valley Railway** which offers an eighteen-mile round trip to Wroxham along the River Bure and past woods and pastures. The station is on Norwich Road and has a café and model train shop. The Aylsham hoard was made in July 1968 prior to the building of a new housing estate at Sir William's Close. It consists primarily of Late Bronze Age metalwork in the forms of spearheads, swords and axes.

North of Aylsham, on the way to Holt, are the remains of **Baconsthorpe Castle**, managed by English Heritage. It embodies the story of the rise and fall of one family in particular, **the Heydons**. John Heydon, born in 1479, (he changed his name from Baxter to disguise his lowly origins) was a prosperous lawyer who began the outer gatehouse. His son, Sir Henry Heydon, born in 1504, completed the castle. He also converted part of the castle into a wool-producing factory, as we would call it today. Vast wealth accrued but the Heydons were not good businessmen and accumulated debts resulting in the selling-off of some of the estate from the late sixteenth century. Much of the castle was demolished to pay off money owed, but the outer gatehouse was occupied as a private dwelling until 1920.

There is reported to be a ghostly soldier who, apparently bored, throws stones into the moat from the castle walls. He is not a threatening presence.

This is a beautiful spot to visit, but car owners need to be careful as some of the entry track can be quite deeply rutted.

It is claimed that fabulous finds have been made at Baconsthorpe. In June 1878, men ploughing a field came across maybe 9,000 coins although it is not possible to be precise as many were made off with immediately; the estimated figure primarily derives from an examination of the pots in which the coins were contained. A separate discovery was made a few years later:

...a large pot, containing, it is estimated, not less than 17000 coins was unearthed in 1884. They were of brass and billon, tinned and silvered, and ranged as far as could be ascertained (for many had disappeared before attention was drawn to the find) from Nerva to Aurelian. Such a hoard is scarcely likely to have been a private one, and conjecture is at fault as to the cause of its deposit...[26]

Medieval pottery has been discovered in **Hempstead**, just west of Baconsthorpe.

Baconsthorpe Castle is five miles from the handsome market town of **Holt,** which has some fine buildings and a surprisingly large range of excellent shops. Described by the national press in 1900 as 'a very pleasant little place', it has been completely rebuilt since a fire in May 1708 destroyed the greater part of it. It is the home town to adjacent Greshams School. Greshams lost over 100 old boys in the Great War, said to be an agony for the headmaster, George Howson, who died in 1919 'spent in grief'.

Travelling onward to the coast will bring you to the village of **Glanford** which is a model village built at the beginning of the twentieth century by Sir Alfred Jodrell. It has Dutch-style gabled houses and a purpose-built museum – the **Shell Museum** – which has a collection of shells accumulated by Sir Alfred over sixty years, along with fossils and local archaeological finds. Just up the road is the 110-year-old **Letheringsett Watermill** which is Norfolk's only flour-producing watermill and is very popular with visitors for its magical riverside setting and guided tours. Sir Michael Savory's **Muckleburgh Collection** is along the road near the coast at Weybourne; this is the largest privately owned military museum in the United Kingdom.

In this part of the county, the Broads increasingly beckon as you travel east. **The Norfolk Broads** cover, according to the official website (see below) only 0.1 per cent of the UK, but contain more than a quarter of its rarest wildlife. The waterways include a collection of seven rivers – the Ant, Bure, Thurne, Yare, Wensum, Waveney and Chet – that cut through over 100 square miles of wetland and feed sixty-three inland lakes. At their shallowest they can be only several feet in depth, and were formed by the excavation of peat from at least Roman times, and thereafter by the monks who needed fuel in this cold and often inhospitable landscape. The government of the day was sporadically interested in the area – for instance, an Act of Parliament in March 1670 led

Sailing on the River Bure, Norfolk Broads

to improvements in the locks at Geldeston, Ellingham and Wainford. Again, laws were passed in April 1773 and May 1812 to build locks and excavate the rivers to enable easier passage of wherries. The coming of the railways further decimated trade with some sections of the waterways, for example at Aylsham, being abandoned from 1912.

The Victorians took to boating here in large numbers for their holidays, as well as to swimming in Cromer and taking the pure air in Poppyland. At this time people assumed that The Broads were a natural phenomenon like the pingos of Breckland. The influential Ward Locke guide to the area is telling its readers in 1921 that the Broads 'were probably formed, long ago, by the overflow of the sluggish rivers into the flat surrounding lands', and it was not until the 1960s that Dr Joyce Lambert proved they were man-made. Peat digging and selling was big business and it has been estimated that Norwich Cathedral alone bought 320,000 tons a year.

Usually, people talk of the northern and the southern Broads – the latter being below the A47 cutting across the county and leading into Great Yarmouth.

There, spreading its great sheet of water, far and bright and smooth, on the right hand and on the left – there, as pure in its spotless blue, as still in its heavenly peacefulness as the summer sky above, was the first of the Norfolk Broads.

Wilkie Collins in Armadale, 1866.

Of the Northern Broads, the most famous is Hickling Broad, 320 acres which begin at Potter Heigham, where many choose to start their boating adventure. Thereafter, a mixture of road and river travel can lead you to many villages, inns and eateries. You can hire a boat by the day or week, or buy one if you like, slow right down to 4 mph, listen to the sounds of wildlife and water lapping on the boughs, rustling reeds and soft breezes and marvel at ancient

'Ricking the reed', from Peter Henry Emerson's first photographic album Life and Landscape on the Norfolk Broads, 1886

stone bridges and flint churches as you progress. It is an opportunity to see, hear and breath in a timeless landscape. Norfolk naturalist, Ted Ellis, called the Broads, 'The breathing place for the cure of souls.'

> A whispering and watery Norfolk sound,
> Telling of all the moonlit reads around
>
> Sir John Betjeman

For information on renting or buying a boat, see the Broads Authority website. The site also advises on everything from tolls and insurance to kayaking, and even flying drones.

A Norfolk man, who was also a founder member of the Norfolk Broads Protection Society, was Walter Rye (1843–1929). He was an antiquary who addressed the Norfolk and Norwich Archaeological Society in ebullient fashion – see Archaeological Journals for a written record – campaigned to

If you have a head for heights you can climb to the top of St Helen's Church Tower (eighty-nine steps, two ladders and a trap door) in Ranworth for a stunning view of Ranworth Broad and the River Bure

save several historic buildings in Norwich, wrote over eighty works on the county, has been called 'the father of cross-country running' (he won over 100 cups and titles himself), was athletics correspondent for the *Sporting Gazette*, brought up seven sons and three daughters, and was mayor of Norwich 1908–9. His best-known quote is probably about his wife: he said she was 'the prettiest and pluckiest creature I have ever met'. He was famously scathing about Happisburgh (see Cloudesley Walks to Work: Appendix 1).

Walter Rye wrote the bestseller *A Month on the Norfolk Broads* in 1887 and in it tells the proverbial tale of a person who refused to leave his boat for an hour when sailing in Hickling in case someone should, in his absence, steal a bucket of water from the Broad, and thus cause his craft to be stranded; the intention of the anecdote was to emphasise just how shallow is the Broad at this point!

The Museum of the Broads is at Stalham at the northern end of the Broads. It has a great deal of well-presented information on the people who lived here and has special fun events for children. It is closed November to March.

Woodbastwick village makes for a pleasing detour while exploring the Norfolk Broads, with beautiful nineteenth-century cottages. It is also home to Woodfordes Brewery and Pub, who have been brewing local ales for over thirty years, including the famous 'Nelson's Revenge', and have an on-site shop where you can purchase fine beers, cider, wine and Norfolk food produce.

BeWILDerwood in Horning is a magical adventure trail for children of all ages and adults, too – jungles, zip wires, treehouses and beautiful scenery await.

A Bronze Age find was made at **Barton Turf** in 2016 by an amateur treasure hunter, David Lovett, and reported in the national press. It contains axes, chisels, knives, spears and a hair lock that may be over 80 per cent gold. The finder says that he had searched the field before but this time he concentrated on the centre which had not been previously possible as it had been occupied by grazing animals. The British Museum is buying the hoard.

Among literally thousands of photo opportunities, probably none attracts more tourists than **Thurne Mill**. It was built in the early 1800s and finished its working life in 1936 but has since been restored to glory. You can take a look inside for free and may consider becoming a Friend of Thurne Mill to keep the beautiful sails turning.

Next to the church of St Fabian and Sebastian in Woodbastwick is a flywheel and crank pump

Thurne Mill, Norfolk Broads

Nearby, outside the village of Ludham, is the site of **St Benet's Abbey**, probably the first Benedictine monastery to be built in Norfolk, by King Cnut in AD 1020. This area, remote in the extreme, had been lived in by Christian hermits – a chapel was erected here in about AD 800 by a religious recluse called Suneman. Despite the king's patronage – he gave the monastery three manors – further rebuilding including permission to crenellate in 1327 (creating defensive walls) and some records suggest attempts to encourage veneration around St Margaret of Holme and the relics of Suneman himself, the monastery never grew very numerous, reaching a peak in 1514 with twenty-four monks resident. Sir John Falstof, who built Caister, gave money. Monks from here were some of the diggers of the peat that created the Norfolk Broads. By a combination of chance circumstances, poverty being one, it became the only monastery in England to escape dissolution by Henry VIII and today the Bishop of Norwich is still the titular abbot, leading an annual service on the site. A large wooden cross has been erected where the high altar used to be and it is here that the service takes place. The abbey was abandoned from 1545 and much of the stone taken away in 1579.

St Benet's Abbey Gatehouse

St Benet's Abbey remains and wooden cross

There is a story that a monk in St Benet's Abbey suffered a punishment caused 'by an undue attachment to his bed in the morning'. As was often the case in ecclesiastic affairs, he could obtain dispensation by payment of a fee, but as he was penniless, he had to apply the magic arts in an attempt to come by a fortune. This once again draws attention to the practice of magic, especially alchemy (see: Binham Priory) and necromancy by abbots and monks in medieval Norfolk.

Notes and contact details

Diss – a wonderful and evocative 1964 portrait of Diss made for TV and featuring Sir John Betjeman is now available free on Youtube: *Something about Diss* parts 1 and 2.

Banham Zoo, www.banhamzoo.co.uk 01953 887771

Bressingham Steam and Gardens, www.bressingham.co.uk 01379 686900.

Norfolk Tank Museum, www.norfolktankmuseum.co.uk. Tel: 07703 337714.
Open Tuesday, Wednesday, Thursday and Sunday Easter to end October; 10 am to 5 pm.

Market Cross, Wymondham, www.south-norfolk.gov.uk Tel: 01953 604721.

Mid-Norfolk Railway. www.mnr.org.uk Tel: 01362 690633.

Wymondham Abbey. office@wymondhamabbey.org.uk Tel: 01953 607062.

Wymondham Heritage Museum, www.wymondhamheritagemuseum. co.uk 01953 600205.

Venta Icenorum, www.visitengland.com

Bishop Bonner's Cottage Museum of local history is open on some days of the week. It is run by Dereham Antiquarian Society.

Gressenhall Farm and Workhouse, museums@norfolk.gov.uk or gressenhall.museum@norfolk.gov.uk Tel: 01362 860563. 24-hour recorded information 01362 869263

Dinosaur Adventure Park, Lenwade, www.dinosauradventure.co.uk Tel: 01603 876310.

Blickling Hall, www.nationaltrust.org.uk Tel: 01263 738030.

Bure Valley Railway, www.bvrw.co.uk Tel: 01263 733858.

Letheringsett Watermil,l www.letheringsettwatermill.co.uk
    Tel: 01263 713153.

Muckleburgh Collection, www.muckleburgh.co.uk Tel: 01263 588210.

Norfolk Broads, www.broads-authority.gov.uk Tel: 01603 610734.
    Offices are at Yare House, 62-64 Thorpe Road, Norwich NR1 1RY.

Museum of the Broads, www.northnorfolk.org/museumofthebroads
    Tel: 01692 581681.

Bewilderwood www.bewilderwood.co.uk. Tel: 01603 783900 Check
    times of opening before coming as it is closed during some parts of
    the year and days of the week.

Thurne Mill, info@thurnemill.org.uk Tel: 077967864.

St Benet's Abbey, www.stbenetsabbey.org It is managed by the Norfolk
    Archaeological Trust www.norfarchtrust.org.uk The abbey is off
    the A1062 south from Ludham. If sailing on the Broads, there is a
    mooring very close by.

CHAPTER 4

Norwich and Norfolk Through Time

Stone Age to Norman Conquest

The Roman poet Lucretius, in the first century AD, is probably responsible for the classification of man's ancient history into three periods – the Stone Age, Bronze Age and Iron Age. His great work, lost for hundreds of years and rediscovered in the early fifteenth century within a German monastery, was *De Rerum Natura*, roughly translated as *On the Nature of Things*. He had a great deal to say about early man, pointing out that the first weapons were hands, nails and teeth, and that society developed most effectively and made leaps of progress, such as developing the iron sword, when it adapted to, and learnt from, the limitations of nature. He said:

Trees don't live in the sky, and clouds don't swim
In the salt seas, and fish don't leap in wheatfields,
Blood isn't found in wood, nor sap in rocks.
By fixed arrangement, all that lives and grows
Submits to limit and restrictions.

The first of Lucretius' specified periods, the Stone Age, is seen as lasting from about 3.4 million years ago until 8,000 to 3,000 BC. It was during this time that Norfolk flint was invaluable for weapons, tools and building – the other-worldly craters of Grimes Graves, details of which are given in Chapter 3, date from the later part of this period.

An important find of this era – flint tools, probably to catch and kill animals that were eaten, such as reindeer – was during construction of Norwich City football ground. In another unusual excavation, a Norfolk

These two Lower Palaeolithic hand axes were found on Happisburgh beach by Matt Stevens in 2018 and 2019. Likely age 500,00–600,000 years old

quarry has yielded evidence of a possible Stone Age killing site with mammoth and flint tools, including one hand axe that is actually inside a mammoth skull, along with piles of tusks which must have been gathered intentionally. This has aroused international attention especially as previous sites of this nature were on the Continent.

As regards Stone Age food, before farms first appeared people had no milk or grain and would have eaten what they could hunt or gather. It is believed by nutritionists that the amount of animal protein eaten by early Stone Age man would be impossible for us to digest today as the liver could not cope. Meat or fish could have been fermented – i.e. allowed to rot underground – which would have had a similar effect to cooking, in terms of breaking it down. It has been suggested that during the Ice Age, food was also fermented under water. The meat or fish varied completely from place to place – we have already referred to Norfolk-man eating reindeer and mammoth: he also hunted rhinoceros. Fish was probably harpooned, although there are indications of fishing nets made of twined birch bark and similar materials. In addition, people collected everything possible – plants (evidence from material gathered from between the teeth shows that Stone Age man ate water lilies and herbs) – rodents, birds, insects, beetles, grasshoppers, moths, birds' eggs, flowers, carrots and nuts.

A game-changer was the invention of stone tools to slice and crush meat. This made chewing and digesting much easier. Some time during the Stone Age period man also learnt how to harness and then make fire – scholars differ as to exactly when, but some say from a million years ago, while others put the figure at about 400,000 years ago. Generally, fire being started by striking flint is considered as coming before fire made by wood friction, although this is not universally agreed.

With the advent of bronze and iron-working, flint became obsolete for making implements but continued to be used extensively for building from small workers' homes to public buildings, churches, manor houses and castles. It was also needed to fire guns up to and after the Napoleonic wars; gun flints from the Brandon area were seen as the best in the world. Flint is still a major building material today, especially for housing, and the streets of some new developments, such as Riverside development in Norwich, are paved with it.

During the last part of the Stone Age in Norfolk, from about 4,500 BC, man ceased to be only a hunter-gatherer and began to settle in semi-permanent communities, grow crops and raise animals. This would have meant a redefining of his relationship with the land, of the concept of land ownership and of 'belonging' to certain groups and areas. Evidence of this is seen most clearly in the long barrows to inter the dead. There is material both from mixed burials – where there are remains of more than one person – and from those of individuals. There may well have been mortuary areas where the deceased were left to decompose in the open before being interred in a closed barrow. Proof is rare as the barrows have usually been flattened by ploughing, but one which is undisturbed is at Ditchingham on the Norfolk border near Bungay in Suffolk. It is 35 yards long and just over 6 ft high and is thought it may contain burial chambers, cremation pyres and piles of household rubbish – pots, flints, animal bones etc. Often, it is necessary to go up in a plane to spot barrows; one such found in this way is at Roughton, south of Cromer.

This tendency to settle, own valuable objects and defend possessions increased during the Bronze Age when the alloying of copper with zinc or tin to make brass or bronze led to the creation of artefacts that was previously impossible – everything from hair pins to agricultural tools to helmets and spears. The largest Bronze Age hoard yet discovered was at Isleham, near Ely in Cambridgeshire in 1959 when William 'Bill' Houghton and his brother, Arthur, unearthed 6,500 worked and unworked pieces including swords, arrows, spears, daggers and armour. Some of these items can be seen in the West Stow Anglo-Saxon Village outside Bury St Edmunds, while others are held by the University of Cambridge.

A remarkable Norfolk discovery, the so-called Rudham Dirk, is a middle Bronze Age dagger ploughed up in East Rudham. The landowner did not realise what he had found initially and was going to throw it into a skip before deciding to keep it as a doorstop. It has now been purchased at a cost of £41,000 and can be seen in Norwich Castle Museum. It is nine-tenths copper and one tenth tin (the latter probably from Cornwall).

Changes in burial practices in the Bronze Age led to round barrows becoming the norm. They usually consist of a central mound surrounded by one or more ditches. Archaeologists often refer to the differing shapes as bowl, bell, disc or saucer. Sometimes a large barrow is surrounded by a number of smaller ones, forming a kind of Bronze Age cemetery. One site like this is at Salthouse Heath. Another is the Bell Hill Bronze Age round barrow at Little Cressingham. The first barrow of the period in Norwich to be discovered is under Ber Street.

Norwich Southern Bypass was built allowing for the excavation of several barrows, the existence of which had been known for some time, but it was obviously a 'now or never' situation here. In addition, in 2016, construction work on the bypass was held up while a late Bronze Age settlement with between eight and ten buildings was found. Pottery, struck flint, burnt flint and a complete fired-clay spindle-whorl were on the 2 hectare site. What makes it unique in Britain, however, is that the buildings in the 'village' are separated by post-holes and not ditches.

Cremation became common during the end of the Bronze Age and there are correspondingly less barrows from this period onwards.

The Iron Age led to hammering and not just casting of materials with an increase in ornamentation and curvilinear construction. Food growing witnessed the introduction of the iron plough and other iron implements of complex design.

Warham Camp is one of the best preserved iron age hill forts in East Anglia

A spectacular discovery of Iron Age gold coins, or staters, was found in 2003 by the Sedgeford Historical and Archaeological Research Project (SHARP) hidden in the bone of a cow's leg. Evidence of an Iron Age settlement, in the form of 200 skeletons, was simultaneously discovered at this time along the valley of the Heacham River.

Tribal leaders were increasingly able to look at the landscape and work with it to build structures and settlements that were advantageous from a defensive point of view. During the Iron Age the dominant tribe in Norfolk was the Iceni and excavations suggest sites with forts in many places – at Thetford, Nuns Bridges, Saham Toney, Micklemoor Hill, Holkham, Warham, Bloodgate Hill and Tasburgh among the most notable. They were built where a natural feature supplied defensive advantage and thus took many forms, although ramparts and ditches were added, and none are very large by the standards of other forts in England.

No defensive structures or weapons were a match for the Romans, however, and when the armies of Julius Caesar encountered resistance in the AD 40s, they decided to disarm the local tribes and the Iceni, under Prasutagus, husband of Boudica, was ineffective against the professional Roman soldier – he was finally defeated, possibly at Holkham. He continued to rule as a vassal king. A network of roads, north to south and east to west, was established, the most famous being the Peddars Way, facilitating rapid troop deployment in the case of trouble.

> So the Queen Boadicea, standing loftily charioted,
> Brandishing in her hand a dart and rolling glances lioness-like,
> Yell'd and shriek'd between her daughters in her fierce volubility.
>
> Alfred Lord Tennyson

This well-ordered Roman world was thrown into confusion with Boudica's rebellion (some spell her name 'Boudicea') in AD 60. When her husband, Prasutagus died, one version of the story has it that his will, which had laid down that the region should be ruled by Boudica and her daughters, was ignored, Boudica beaten and the daughters raped. Another version maintains that the Roman financier, Seneca, called in loans he had made to Prasutagus and which could not be repaid. At the time, most of the Roman army was fighting outside East Anglia subduing the Druids of Wales. As the campaign began, Boudica quickly sacked the Roman settlements of Colchester, London and St Albans, killing an estimated 70,000 to 80,000 Romans and English – anyone there, irrespective of nationality, was liable to slaughter – but the main Roman army fought back and crushingly defeated her at the Battle of Watling Street. She then either died or took her own life, subsequent Roman writers differing in their accounts. So shaken was the Roman Emperor Nero by these events that he briefly considered quitting Britain altogether. Over the centuries, Boudica, Queen of Iceni, became a folk hero with pubs, a magazine, streets, cafés and all sorts named after her and her tribe in Norfolk to this day.

The Romans built many forts which typically were shaped like rectangles with rounded corners and a gateway in the centre of each side. Some were quite large containing barracks, workshops, stores and stables – Saham Toney fort for example could house 800 soldiers. From AD 200 the Romans also fortified many towns, Caistor St Edmund being rebuilt in stone with walls 11ft thick. Others were fortified to varying degrees and much has been discovered about these by metal detection, which has unearthed iron artefacts and led to the discovery of pottery and other everyday non-metal items at settlements that include Brampton, Walsingham and Billingford on the River Wensum. Sometimes these were shore forts, principal examples being Brancaster, Caister-next-Yarmouth and Burgh Castle.

Clues to life and diet can be obtained at the sites of Roman burials where the bones still survive, but until very recently these were rare in Norfolk, numbering only about 300. In 2012, however, the BBC reported that eighty-five graves had been discovered in Great Ellingham, near Attleborough, dating from the third and fourth century, with some of those buried having been decapitated after death – the head was placed between the feet. There is also evidence of flints having been deliberately placed around some of the heads.

Prior to the Great Ellingham discovery, there was little evidence of Roman burials. One, however, was made in the nineteenth century at Norwich:

A discovery of considerable Archaeological interest was made on 2 December 1861, in a chalk pit, the property of Mr Bassett, at Stone Hills in the parish of Heigham … about four ft below the surface, a coffin of lead, which had been enclosed in a wooden one … No external ornamentation was visible. Within, the remains of a female skeleton were found. The

A Roman Centurion features on the Anmer village sign

The remains of the walls at Venta Icenorum, Caistor St Edmund

jawbones were entire, and the teeth well preserved, the shape and enamel of the latter very beautiful ... I am not aware of any similar discovery having been made in Norfolk ... but my enquiries lead me to suggest a Roman burial.[27]

When the Romans left, according to Francis Blomefield's *Topographical history of the county of Norfolk, etc*:

> The Britons being ruined of all their strength by the Romans continually carrying off their youth, and now abandoned by their garrisons, which alone could have supported the declining state, fell into miserable confusions, and terrible calamities, occasioned by the barbarian invasions on the one hand, and the tumultuous factions of their great men on the other, striving for the supreme government, everyone being for usurping it for himself.

In 654 king of the East Angles, Anna, was killed at the Battle of Blythburgh with his daughter, Withburga, fleeing to Dereham where she established a nunnery. Her story is recounted in Chapter 3. The Danes invaded under their leader, Ivar the Boneless who defeated King Edmund at the Battle of Hoxne.

Wooden baying wolf sculpture at Old Hunstanton

Folklore

The legend of King Edmund is commemorated in Hunstanton, where he also appears on the town sign. By the lighthouse in Old Hunstanton and on a spectacular part of the Norfolk Coast Walk there is a wooden baying wolf sculpture. The story goes that, following his defeat, King Edmund was offered his life if he denounced Christ; he refused, was shot through with arrows and decapitated, his body and head being thrown into a nearby wood. His broken-hearted subjects soon managed to find the body, but not being able to locate the head, one of them cried out: 'Where are you? Where are you?' The cry came back 'Hic! Hic! Hic!' (old English for 'Here! Here! Here!') The head was found guarded by a wolf who permitted the search party to take it back to the body.

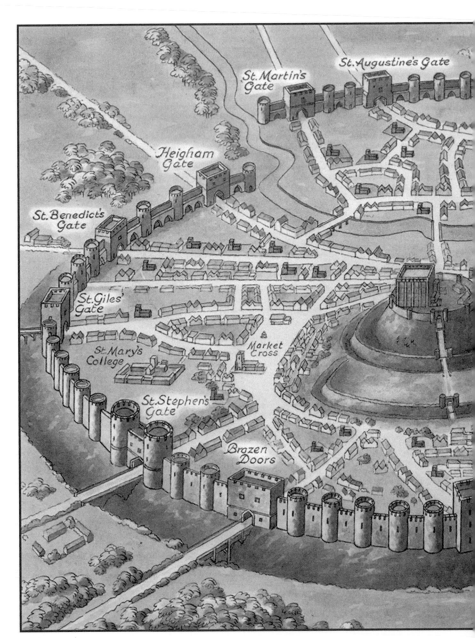

A modern illustration of how Norwich would have looked in the fourteenth century, complete with its medieval walls and towers. Courtesy of Aviva Archive. Norwich Union commissioned an artist named Tom Griffiths in the early 1950s to produce this fine map

Magdalen
Gate

Mousehold
Heath

Barre
Gate

White
Friars
Priory

Cow Tower

St Giles (Great
Hospital)

Bishop
Gate

Cathedral

Tombland

Grey Friars
Priory

Austin Friars
Priory

Boom
Towers

Conisford
Gate

Black
Tower

Tom Griffiths

Norwich

Norwich as it may be recognised today dates from the eighth century (the very first settlement was probably around the time of the Iceni dominance about AD 43 when it was known as Northwic); it certainly has evidence of Danish earthwork defences. The first part to be occupied was possibly Magdalen Street, leading to a wooden crossing at Fye Bridge; there is also Danish influence in some of the church construction. The previous Roman Road through Norwich was parallel to this – Oak Street into Coslany; the route is typically straight. Danish rule lasted only for about fifty years and when it ended, from AD 917, Oak Street developed as a metalworking area, the river at this time which runs alongside being busy with trading craft. Later, prior to the Great War and at the end of the period covered in this study, this same area would become the worst slum in the city, the epicentre of cloth-dying and beer production, street names today in this now completely rebuilt and affluent area – Dyer Court, Indigo Yard – reflecting these times. It was Thetford, however, that was the most influential part of Norfolk during this period, before power and influence shifted, along with the establishment of the cathedral at Norwich by Herbert de Losinga in 1094.

By AD 939 Norvic had its own mint, the word being found on coins across Europe at this time. To this day the Bishop of Norwich signs himself 'Norvic'. The Domesday Book in 1086 records that the city had twenty-five churches and a population of between 5,000 and 10,000. Many inhabitants would have been from Scandinavia as Quern stones (stones for hand-grinding), which have been found recently during excavations in the city centre, bear witness.

The Danes

There is evidence of defences being constructed at the Red Castle in Thetford around AD 700 and of a wooden church dedicated to St Lawrence. The Danes fortified it after AD 900 with banks and ditches and it was further strengthened as the century progressed, but these could not save it from being sacked and looted by Swein Forkbeard in AD 1004.

In the tenth century power ebbed and flowed between the Danes and Saxons, by no means all Danish expeditions being as successful as the mythical term

'Viking Conquest' suggests. However, in AD 999 Swein Forkbeard, King of Denmark, fought and defeated his previous commander, Olaf, who had embraced Christianity and rebelled. He now turned on East Anglia and threatened Norwich with his fleet. An attempt to destroy his fleet was repulsed but he was attacked again on retreat from the sacking of Thetford and only escaped having lost much of his booty. Six years passed during which East Anglia was ruled by the victor of this campaign, a man called Ulfcytel. In AD 1013, however, Swein Forkbeard launched an invasion of all of England, installing his son, Cnut, as king. King Cnut then attacked Norwich and in 1016 won a decisive battle against his enemies. He reigned for two decades.

In English folklore King Cnut is remembered as the man who sat on a beach and ordered the waves to retreat, but this story is probably myth. His legacy is overshadowed by what happened soon after, historically speaking – the Norman Conquest. Many historians, however, call him 'Cnut the Great', reflected in the description that he gave himself and which survives in a letter: 'King of all England and Denmark and the Norwegians and of some of the Swedes'.

The Norman Conquest and aftermath

The Normans brought castles to Britain. Prior to their arrival, and subsequently sometimes, a thegn – a member of the aristocratic class – would often build a residential compound with defensive features, called a burh-geat ('burh' means 'fortification'). Some were primarily castles with living space, and some more houses with defensive features added. A magnificent fifteenth-century example of the latter is Baconsthorpe Castle. There were also many churches with defensive features. Some parts of Norfolk had insufficient stone for building and utilised flint; this is the most probable reason for the existence still of 119 round tower churches in the county – it was difficult to construct the buttresses needed for square towers without stone. Where stone was needed for prestigious projects, such as the building of Norwich Cathedral, it needed to be imported from other parts of England or from overseas locations like Caen.

Initially, Norman castles were of earth and timber with a high 'motte', i.e. mound, a prime example being at Thetford – other locations in Norfolk

The Saxon-built round tower of St Mary's, Burnham Deepdale

include Denton and Middleton. At Thetford, the castle was superimposed on an earlier Iron Age fort. That it has not survived is probably due to the fact that the town quickly became secondary to Norwich at the end of the eleventh century and the wooden structure was never upgraded into stone.

Norwich Castle was built on a different scale to anything that had gone before. Its primary purpose would have been to show where authority lay. Perhaps ninety houses were demolished around the site and a large part of the original castle was buried to form the great mound, the purpose of which was to bear the weight of the keep. It may have been started about the same time as the cathedral, and that it was completed fairly quickly is suggested by the fact that the complete castle is represented by the master masons and artists who built the cathedral as the kingdom of heaven, i.e. the grandest vision they had ever seen. This would suggest, although historians differ, that it was completed before the visit of Henry I in 1109 when the stonemasons were creating the magnificent bosses on the cathedral roof.

The castle was at the forefront of national events almost immediately when Ralf Guader, the Earl of Norfolk, proposed a marriage to Countess Emma

Norwich Castle Bridge

and found himself out of favour in consequence of it being unacceptable to the new masters. However, he returned from exile, had his lands restored, married Emma in 1075 and tried to raise an army against the king. Emma retreated to the castle and held out against a siege for three months, but was finally forced to surrender to Archbishop Lanfranc who granted her safe passage to Brittany. The king, however, did not forgive Ralf Guader, imprisoning him and taking various actions against those who had either been at the wedding or in the rebel army.

Again, in 1088, there was a plot by the governor of the castle, Roger Bigod, and others to replace King William with his brother, Robert, Duke of Normandy, but it faded away quickly.

The Anarchy is a period in English history between 1135 and 1153 when law and order largely broke down and was a turbulent time for Norwich. It was precipitated by a succession crisis. Henry I had decreed that his daughter, Maud, should succeed him, but her cousin, Stephen, seized the throne. Norwich Castle was held at this time by Hugh Bigod who supported Maud, but Stephen was able to secure a marriage between his son William, who was made Earl of Norfolk, and the de Warenne heiress. Meanwhile, at Castle Rising, the d'Albinis flew Stephen's colours. An agreement was reached in 1153 which saw Maud's son take the throne as Henry II.

It was in this period that Jews began arriving in Norwich and in 1144 they were accused of the ritual murder of the boy William of Norwich, who quickly acquired the status of martyr and was canonised. Miracles were declared at the place where his body had been found and some pilgrims – not very many probably – made offerings at the cathedral. In February 1190 all the Jews of Norwich that could not find refuge in the cathedral were massacred. In 2004, workmen clearing ground for the new shopping centre found a well which contained the bones of seventeen people, including eleven children, with subsequent DNA tests confirming that they were all related, perhaps members of the Ashkenazi Jewish family.

Thirty years later, Henry II faced a crisis when Henry Bigod, Earl of Norfolk, attacked and took Norwich Castle in support for Prince Henry, who was seeking to take the throne from his father. The rebels were subsequently defeated near Bury St Edmunds and Henry II razed Thetford Castle.

The Dauphin of France took the castle again in 1216 in support of the rebellion against King John. King John took his army to King's Lynn later in the year, but died of dysentery.

The remains of Simon de Montfort's defeated army – he had risen against Henry III – looted King's Lynn and Norwich in 1263, taking 100 wagons of loot to Ely and Henry sent a force to finally end the rebellion.

Castle Rising keep was built from 1138 to rival Norwich Castle. William d'Albini, whose family traditionally occupied Old Buckenham Castle, married Adeliza, the widow of Henry I, and set about creating a complex that included a castle, deer park, warren, and town. The dimensions, construction and finish bear many similarities to Norwich.

Castle Acre had a complex beginning. Originally, in AD 1085, it seems to have been a house inside an unusual circular ringwork without strong defences; by 1140 there appears to have been a rethink with various defensive measures taken, including doubling the thickness of the outer walls and erecting a shell keep.

At about the same time, William d'Albini was erecting the first circular stone keep in England at Old Buckenham Castle. Other structures that were

NORWICH AND NORFOLK THROUGH TIME   227

built of stone at this time in Norfolk were Walter de Cadamo's Horsford motte, the Fitzalans' castle at Mileham, the castle at Weeting built for Sir Ralf de Plais and Marham Castle.

1300–1455

The Black Death killed half the population of Norwich 1348–9, 1361–2, 1369 and 1379–83. Francis Blomefield, the eighteenth century historian already quoted, puts the deaths in the city in the first of these periods at over 5,000. In the Anglican Cathedral there is graffiti among which there are people's initials carved inside representations of churches, and elsewhere sailing ships feature – this may well be from this period denoting a wish for safety and to sail away from terrible times (more details and pictures in the authors' book *Spirit of Norwich Cathedral*, PiXZ). There was great lawlessness as life was so cheap, but paradoxically, the Great Plague, as it is sometimes called, led to a substantial rise in the wage of the working man, as they were so scarce, something that was not reversed when the sickness and death ended.

In 1377 the French invaded and pillaged ports on the south coast and this led to increased fortifications of all Norfolk towns. Castle Rising gained prominence, and extra defensive features after it was occupied by Isabella, widow of Edward II and partner of the usurper Mortimer – some historians say that she was actually imprisoned here – in 1331 until she died in 1358. It is part of local folklore that she can still sometimes be seen roaming the battlements at night.

The '100 Years' War', 1337–1453, between England and France over rights to the French throne and other disputes, made this a period of great uncertainty and various constables in Norwich, Castle Rising and elsewhere in Norfolk were empowered to conscript men for the army. Some, however, made fortunes by looting in France and capturing and then ransoming French aristocrats. One such was Sir John Fastolf who built Caister Castle, unusually built of brick, between 1432 and 1446. Baconsthorpe Castle was another notable building started in this period by John Heydon. It has a fine moat and these became very fashionable for defensive, practical (keeping fish for food) and aesthetic reasons; it has been estimated that there were over 200 moated properties in Norfolk at the end of the fifteenth century.

If you wished to have battlements on your new building, it was necessary to obtain a licence to crenelate.

It was also considered imperative to improve the defensive walls of King's Lynn – one of the wealthiest towns in the country during this period – Great Yarmouth, and, of course, Norwich. The right to levy an extra tax, a so-called murage grant, could be applied for by the authorities just for this purpose. The walls of Norwich were mainly completed by 1344 and some parts, such as a very fine stretch existing at the top of Bracondale, can still be visited. Other remnants, such as those alongside Chapelfield Shopping centre, can also be seen.

In the latter part of the fourteenth century, life could be very hard for the average agricultural worker. Food was scarce with hated warren lodges, such as that at Thetford, guarding the rabbit population for the sole enrichment of the landowner, and, such was the rampant corruption that unless you had money, there was no recompense for injustice and many landowners made life almost impossible for their workers. Worst of all, to many were the seemingly endless taxes imposed to pay for the war with France, which was not even going well. There was a tax imposed in 1371, another in 1377, a third in 1379 – amounting to as much as three days' wages – and finally an announcement that there would be a further tax in 1381.

The Peasants Revolt of 1381 began in London and quickly spread, especially in Norfolk where contemporary records show that 1,214 men became rebels. The leader was a man called Geoffrey Lister and he was supported by some eminent Norfolk knights including Sir Roger Bacon. Together, this varied band took and pillaged Norwich, demanding large sums from wealthy merchants in exchange for not damaging their property or goods. Several despised tax collectors and justices were beheaded.

The revolt was put down primarily by Henry Despenser, who was appointed Bishop of Norwich at the age of 27. Descended from Hugh Despenser, hated favourite of Edward II, he had spent his younger days fighting in Italy and was given the title as a reward from the Pope. He set out to crush the rebellion, killing many in East Anglia (it is often referred to as 'judicial murder' as so many died brutally and unnecessarily) and headed towards Norwich, outside of which Lister tried to make peace. However, Lister's forces were routed by Despenser at North Walsham – the site of the battle is one of only five battlefields in Norfolk that are recognised by Norfolk County Council. Lister was hanged, drawn and quartered in London. A sculpture in the Memorial Park, North Walsham, carved in 1999 by Mark Goldsworthy from the trunk of a 120-year-old oak tree, commemorates the battle. A further conspiracy was uncovered centring on the Abbey of St Benet at Hulme the following year and ten people put to death. Bishop Despenser donated the Despenser Reredos to the Anglican Cathedral in commemoration of the failure of the revolt. It is one of the cathedral's greatest treasures and is on public display today (details under 'Norwich Cathedral' above).

One of the key battles of the 100 Years' War was Agincourt, and this involved Norwich men. Henry V landed in France in August 1415 with an army of 12,000. He firstly besieged the town of Harfleur which surrendered on 22 September. In October he fought the famous battle against a numerically superior French force – accounts vary, but it is usually assumed that he had 1500 men-at-arms and 7,000 longbowmen, while a contemporary historian put the number of the French at 50,000. He didn't want to fight as he was trying to reach Calais so that his exhausted and hungry men could reach home. There was also a mass outbreak of dysentery among the ranks. However, the French blocked his path and he had no alternative but to give battle on 25 October. He ordered that every person remain silent on the night before battle on pain of losing an ear; this was in contrast to the French who, so confident of victory, taunted the English and constructed a specially painted cart in which they intended to parade the defeated British king.

The longbowmen were commanded by Sir Thomas Erpingham from Norwich and many of them had trained in Chapelfield Gardens. Sunday archery training was compulsory for all able-bodied men of the city of Norwich at this time. In the battle the heavily armed French soldiers considered themselves superior fighters and thought that the longbowmen were of little consequence. The muddy conditions made movement very difficult for the soldiers as wave after wave of arrows, fired in an arc high into the sky, descended onto the French army, which was decimated. On many occasions, in the hand-to-hand fighting, all that an English soldier had to do was to push his opponent over into the boggy ground – they were so heavy that they were unable to get up again. The conditions also meant that the famous French cavalry could hardly charge – when they did they encountered sharp poles facing upwards from the ground and this kept the English foot-soldier safe. Henry quickly gained several thousand prisoners, but afraid that they might decide to fight again, he had all but the most noble slaughtered – the reason for sparing these men was that a sizeable ransom could be expected.

It is estimated – though it is impossible to be sure – that between 4,000 and 10,000 Frenchmen were killed, including many of the highest nobles. Maybe 1,600 of Henry's men perished.

There was one victory for the French; an account by an English chaplain recounts a successful attack on the English baggage train during which one of Henry's crowns – he had quite a few – was taken.

Following the victory, many considered Henry V to have been blessed by God and he has passed into English legend. Sir Thomas returned to Norwich a national hero and paid for the Erpingham Gate leading into the cathedral. Look up to see a small stone statue of him in prayer, thanking God for having saved his life. On the other side you can see his coat of arms. He also started St Mary's Church in the Norfolk village of **Erpingham** which was completed after his death.

The 'Agincourt Carol' was written to celebrate the victory. The lyrics of the chorus are:

> Then went hym forth, owre king comely,
> In Agincourt feld he faught manly;
> Throw grace of God most marvelsuly,
> He had both feld and victory.

The dawn of the Tudors

The Wars of the Roses lasted thirty years from 1455 between the rival Houses of York and Lancaster. The final victory on Bosworth Field of Henry, Earl of Richmond, over Richard III ushered in what is known as the Tudor period, lasting until the death of Elizabeth 1 in 1603. This was a chaotic and often lawless time in Norfolk with local bands, affiliated to one lord or other, roaming the county. It saw the eventual rise to great prominence of the

Paston family – Sir John Paston III was Sheriff of Norfolk and Suffolk in 1487 under Henry VII.

In 1549, Kett's Rebellion saw the bloodiest period in Norwich's history (see Chapter 1). At this time and until the Industrial Revolution, Norwich was the largest city in England after London.

At this time occurred what has become known as the 'Norwich Conspiracy of 1570'. In 1565, the mayor and dignitaries of the city were concerned that the worsted manufacturing business had almost collapsed and many houses were standing empty. The queen issued an order allowing up to 30 weavers from the Low Countries to settle in the city. They worshipped at the Black Friars in Elm Hill and at St Mary the Less near Tombland. So successful were the newcomers that a conspiracy was born out of jealousy to expel them from the country. The chief protagonists were named as John Thockmorten, George Redman, John Appleyerde, and a man named only as Naller. When they reached Norwich (from Beccles, Bongay – i.e. Bungay – and Harleston) they were in such a 'sodeyne' – old English word for an impulsive or poorly thought out state of mind – that they stole the city plate to finance their actions. Their cry was: 'We will raise up the commons and levy a power and beat the strangers out of the City of Norwich … And after we have levied our power, we will hang up all such as will not take our parts.' There was, however, no sudden mass movement for which these men had hoped, although a small motley band was raised at Cringleford, which soon dispersed. They were arrested.

At their trial, John Appleyard claimed that he had planned to betray the men all along by inviting them to a banquet and calling soldiers – his motive, he said, was to gain influence with the queen. Another man, of the Kett family, said he had been the informant. Norwich gaol was overflowing and we have records showing that other buildings had to be hired to house all the accused, that the cost of additional warders was £5 a week and that rounding up the traitors had cost the crown a total of £26 13s 4d.

There also exists a list of the food supplied to the Chief Justice and retinue who were summoned from London for the trial which lasted five days. It shows they had: two hogsheads of wine, beer, four steers, twenty-four muttons, seven veals, geese, swans, capons, rabbits, pigeons, chickens, wild fowls, butter, bread, eggs, apples, pears, cherries, quinces and strawberries.

A letter in the British Library from George, Earl of Shrewsbury, says 'the great Sitting is done at Norwich', and confirms that these four were condemned for high treason; they were subsequently 'hanged, drawne and quartered'. As they had been convicted of treason their estates were forfeit to the crown and George Redman's property was given by the queen to the Great Hospital in St Helen's. He is buried in St Peter Mancroft.

One of the newcomers was Anthony de Solempne, not a weaver, but the first printer in the city, and it was he who printed and saved for posterity the final verse of another Norwich conspirator condemned to death. His name was 'Thom. Brooke, Gentleman, of Rollesby, Norfolk', and he was executed on 30 August 1570. The day prior he wrote:

All languishing I lye,
And death doth make me thrall,
To cares which death will sone cut off,
And sett me quyt of all.
Yet feble fleshe would faynt,
To feal so sharpe a fyght,
Save fayth in Christ doth comfort me,
And fleithe such fancy quyght.

The fourth Duke of Norfolk, Thomas Howard, was executed in 1572, at the age of 36, for plotting with Spain to marry Mary, Queen of Scots, and place her on the throne. It is probable that an invasion force from Spain would have landed on the Norfolk coast and marched upon London. Mary would have been his fourth wife. His lands were forfeit for several generations. The duke had set up his palace in Duke Street, Norwich. He is reputed to have said: 'When I am in the tennis court of my palace in Norwich, I think myself as great as the king.'

Spain launched the Armada against England in 1588, but partly through mismanagement and partly bad weather, a third of the 130 ships were lost and the attempted invasion failed. It is reported that the bells of St Peter Mancroft Church rang out to inform the citizens of Norwich of this great deliverance. It was to keep up this tradition, the peals celebrating all future British major victories – Waterloo, Trafalgar and both world wars among them.

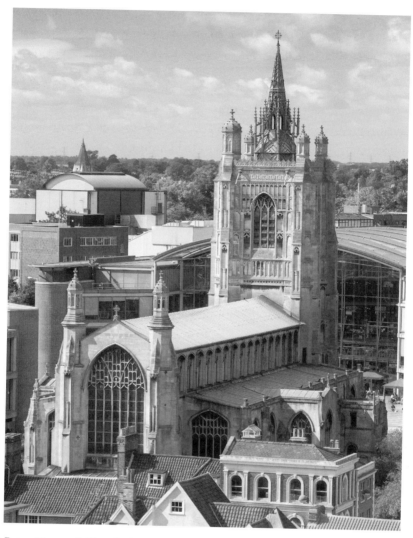

St Peter Mancroft Church, Norwich

One effect of the war was that Flemings fleeing Spanish persecution settled in Norwich bringing their skills in textile working with them along with a more unusual import – the canary. Norwich became the leading breeding centre for the birds and the green and yellow variety has become the emblem of Norwich City Football Club, which is also nicknamed The Canaries.

Attempts, serious at Great Yarmouth, Norwich and King's Lynn, and less so around the coast at Weybourne (or Wayborn as originally written) and other coastal villages, were made to improve defences, mainly by improving walls and supplying guns.

Musket and archery practice became compulsory for Norfolk men in many areas such as Norwich. In Norwich, one area utilised for this purpose was Chapelfield Gardens – the name derives from the fact that there used to be a monastery on the present site of the Theatre Royal where the chapel was called St Mary's, the field adjacent being named Chapel Field.

The importance of Strangers

Norwich has periodically welcomed relatively large numbers of people from overseas who have contributed to local life and culture. One such time was the latter part of the sixteenth century when possibly a third of the population of Norwich was from the Low Countries.

The reason for this particular influx was that anyone denying the Roman Catholic faith in what was then the Spanish Netherlands – this is now the Netherlands, Belgium and some of France – was liable to be persecuted, tortured and killed. Consequently, many Protestants fled to cities such as Norwich with which they had strong trading links. Records show that in 1571 there were almost 4,000 'Strangers' in the city – this, from a total population of probably around 15,000. The number increased to about 6,000 in the next ten years. Most were weavers, wool combers, traders in various goods including wine and gardeners, but a few brought other skills; for example, Anthony de Solempne from Brabant, as above, was the first man to print books in the city after he arrived in 1567.

These people lived in the poorest areas of the city, by and large – King Street and St Benedicts, for example. When plague swept through the city, as it did in 1579, they tended to be especially vulnerable.

There have been many other examples of people from overseas finding a home in Norwich, one of the most notable of this century being the arrival of pilots and their families from Poland during the Second World War. In the twenty-first century, people from countries in the European Union have come over to the city and other areas of Norfolk.

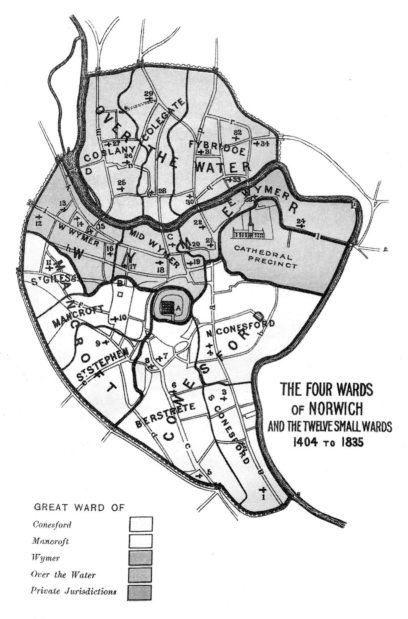

A map of the four wards of Norwich and the twelve smaller wards between 1404 and 1835

Life could be brutal at this time, one way of keeping alive being begging, which on some occasions was sanctioned, even licenced, by the authorities. Although normally a person would be fined, branded or even executed for begging, it was allowed in certain circumstances, for example, if you had lost your goods by fire or at sea, were a university student and needed money to get through the vacations, were a leper (begging allowed by proxy in this case), or had fallen unexpectedly into destitution. It was necessary to have a warrant signed by the Bishop of Norwich or another eminent citizen – we know that William Paston signed some – and the usual term was for a year in order to beg in your own area or adjacent hundreds. Records exist showing that warrants were issued in the late sixteenth century in some areas of Norfolk including the Norwich-Cromer-Yarmouth segment.

The Civil War 1642–51

Norfolk's armed men, under the command of the Duke of Warwick, as well as the navy off the coast, declared for the Parliamentarians at the beginning of the war. East Anglia raised 20,000 men for the New Model Army and the people of Norwich were asked to pay for a troop of cavalry, the famous 'Ironsides'.

King's Lynn was declared a royalist stronghold by the governor, Sir Hamon L'Estrange, in August 1643. He had a force of 2,000 troops and forty guns: the Red Mount chapel was turned into a fort. He did not, however, receive help from the king as expected and in September 1643 surrendered to the Earl of Manchester, who had 4,500 men. The king ordered a futile retaking of Lynn by Sir Roger L'Estrange in 1644.

Norwich had a far from peaceful civil war as many people resented the puritan atmosphere and rioted; eight were executed in Castle Ditch in 1648. There was a royalist plot in 1650, led by Thomas Coke, and the suppression of this led to twenty-five executions.

The decisive turning point in the war was the victory of Cromwell's forces over the royalist army at Naseby on 14 June 1645. Thereafter, Prince Rupert tried to take the battle to the seas which involved harassing the fishing fleet off the Norfolk coast and three men-of-war were stationed at Great Yarmouth to help fend him off.

For 150 years after the Civil War, the Norfolk coast was seen as vulnerable to French invasion, a situation only significantly altered by the defeat of the French at Trafalgar by Norfolk's premier sea hero, Admiral Lord Nelson, in 1805.

I am truly amazed and half alarmed to find the county filled with little Revolutionary Societies.

> Novelist, diarist and playwright, Fanny Burney,
> born in King's Lynn in 1752, writing of Norfolk.

Norwich was wealthy by the beginning of the eighteenth century and this was primarily based on wool and weaving. This is evidenced by the fact that the county as a whole boasted an advanced system of poor relief and in 1771 the Norfolk and Norwich Hospital was founded, paid for mostly by individual subscription. Entertainments were by no means second to London. Harriet Martineau, discussed in Chapter 1, held supper parties for the city's literati and declared herself and friends 'The Athens of England'. It was also a hotbed of discordant groups politically: in 1790 the Blue Bell Inn (later the Bell Hotel) became the meeting place for the newly founded Norwich Revolution Society which by and large stuck to noisy debate. This was followed five years later by the Norwich Patriotic Society. Both of these groups were engaged in rabble-rousing at the notoriously disordered and at times blatantly corrupt Norfolk elections.

Norwich and Norfolk: the Regency era and into the Victorian age

The term Regency is usually taken as referring to the years 1795 to 1837 and includes the reigns of George III, George IV and William IV. It was a period of great social and artistic achievement as well as witnessing, notably in the battles of Nelson and Wellington, the emergence of Britain as the world's unchallenged superpower, a situation that continued during the reign of Queen Victoria (1837–1901). So, how was life as a citizen of Norwich and Norfolk during this transformative time? Fortunately, the local press in the form of the *Norfolk Chronicle and Norwich Gazette* and other newspapers, was also thriving and from sources such as these we can gain a colourful glimpse into daily life in the county.

The population of Norfolk in July 1801 was returned as 274,221 (as opposed to about 898,000 in 2019), of whom 130,249 were males and 143,972 females. About 4,000 men from Norwich were serving in Wellington's army which balances up the figures slightly.

At the outset of this period life was hard for the working man. Napoleon threatened invasion, food was scarce and prices high. On 4 August 1801 the local press advised men to be ready in case of invasion and many reported to St Andrew's Hall to show support. Throughout August of that year many meetings were held in Norfolk to prepare contingency plans.

If life became impossible, the last resort was the workhouse (see Gressenhall Farm and Workhouse, Chapter 3). As Charles Dickens was to write, one of the greatest fears of entering the workhouse was that your body may well be sold upon death for medical purposes, and it was believed that only those in possession of all their bones and organs would be able to

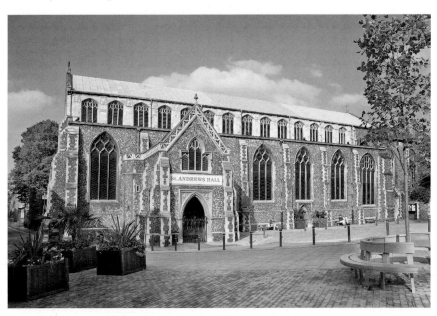

St Andrew's Hall, Norwich

enter the Kingdom of Heaven.[28] People fought hard not to enter and this, combined with a need for men for Wellington's army, meant that workhouses in Norwich were less full in 1801 than a short while previously.

If you became ill, unless money was available, there was very little help. Occasionally, the local authorities would provide a doctor free of charge – to those presenting themselves in the marketplace for daily work, for instance – but medical care was expensive. There were a few burial clubs, the predecessors of private health care, but benefits were limited. If you could afford it, the best thing was to make your own funeral arrangements. One who did this was the parish clerk of St Peter's Terrington who, according to the *Norfolk Chronicle and Norwich Gazette*, had a coffin made which he kept in his bedroom. Even the brass plaque was completed – all that had to be added was the year of death.

Violence, transportations, whippings, duckings (for women) and hangings were a constant feature of existence. There was no police force – such forces as existed were privately funded by local wealthy businessmen and liable to corruption until the first 'official' units began to operate in London from 1829 – and a fact of life was that justice was usually dependent on how much money you could raise: sometimes adverts appeared in the local press seeking money from charitable citizens.

The press of the time was brimming with accounts of executions and other punishments. The following are a few:

Johnstone Wardell, aged 23, was accused of embezzling the sum of £1,431, 18*s* 7*d* from the Bank of England in his role as a bank clerk. He retained a famous lawyer, Mr Kelly, at a cost of 100gs, and was acquitted, claiming that he was robbed on Castle Ditches. Several months later he confessed although he knew he would be hanged.

James Clarke, aged 20, was executed on Castle Hill for setting fire to a haystack. This was despite the 'arrangement' he made with an old man named Wyer, 'well known for his eccentricities' who declared on the Hill that he would take his place for five shillings, 'went home, made good his word, and hanged himself'.

Frances Billing and Catherine Frarey were found guilty of the murder of Mary Taylor by arsenic poisoning and Robert Frarey. They held hands on the scaffold, there was silence in the massed crowd and then a 'piercing shriek', according to a reporter present.

James Johnson, 29, was convicted of slitting the throat of a breeches-maker, Mr Robert Baker. He was found guilty on 19 March 1818 and was ordered to be hanged and his body given over to medical science on the following Saturday. However, he asked the judge to allow more than two days in which to prepare for eternity and the sentence was postponed until the Monday when it was witnessed by a crowd of 5,000 at Castle Hill.

On one occasion, four men's executions were given in a single edition of the local paper. John Allen, 23, and John Day, 26, were hanged in Norwich for burglary at the house of the Rev. Isaac Horley of North Walsham: Day had previously deserted from the British Army on thirteen occasions. Richard Grafton suffered the same fate for stealing a cow and three heifers as did James Chettleburgh for stealing six sheep at Saxlingham – unusually, the last took place at Thetford.

Often, a hanged body would be left for a period in a gibbet. One such was that of a man called Watson who, having been convicted of murdering his wife, was displayed on Bradenham Common near Swaffham. It was ordered to be taken down after a starling, plus young ones, made a nest in his chest and attracted hundreds of onlookers.

Other sentences for lesser crimes could be harsh. John William Smith was sentenced to seven years' transportation for stealing a silver spoon and a coat from two different public houses in Norwich. Thomas Carter was publicly whipped in Norwich Market Place for stealing a cow.

The concept of mental health was gaining serious attention in this era. In Chapter 1, Walk 1, we mention Mary Chapman's pioneering work in establishing a hospital for 'curable lunatics' in Norwich as early as 1728. What happened to those considered incurable is highlighted in a terrible case heard at Norwich where William Frost, aged 35, was found guilty of murdering his four children, aged from 10 weeks to 5 years, by hitting them on the head with a hammer. He was deemed not guilty and sent for life to the Criminal Lunatic Asylum, George's Fields, London.

If life was hard, there were many wonders to witness in this age of great inventions. Flight was beginning to become a possibility – in 1801 it was reported that Mr Green ascended in his balloon in London and descended just outside King's Lynn. Railways were about to transform both business and personal life. In April 1844 the Yarmouth and Norwich Railway was formally opened by Mr R. Stephenson, whose famous *Rocket* had won the Rainhill trials in1829.

Sometimes inventions would seem mundane but had a major impact, such as the invention by the Rev. T.C. Munnings in 1844 and demonstrated at Holkham Fair, of 'a machine for drilling turnips'.

At the end of the Regency period came the first real photographic triumph, the first person in Norwich to advertise 'patent photographic portraits' being Mr Beard, of the Royal Bazaar in 1840. These likenesses were stated to be 'surprisingly correct', and severe chemical tests apparently proved 'that they would last to infinity'. The prices ranged from one to two guineas, which was a huge amount of money and helps explain why surviving images from this period are so valuable.

An invention that seems like a cross between a bicycle and a car was the subject of a court case as reported on 14 October 1843:

In a case before the county justices at the Shirehall, Norwich, in which the keeper of Hellesdon toll-bar was summoned for unlawfully taking toll in respect of a vehicle called a 'wheel machine', interesting particulars were given of the contrivance, which belonged to a Norwich mechanic named Matthew Fish. It was described as 'only a barrow roked by the feet, and not propelled by machinery'. The carriage was shown outside the court, and 'appeared to be a very ingenious machine, which could be worked at the rate of ten miles an hour on a level road'. It had three wheels and two levers … The matter was ultimately settled without a conviction.

There had been an impassioned debate in the eighteenth century as to the wisdom of allowing the working man to read. Many argued that he would become discontent as he was 'designed to go up one furrow and down the

Norwich Thorpe Station and bridge over the River Wensum in 1851

next' and not to think. However, Norwich was the first city outside of London to have a public library. On 4 May 1801 it was reported that the Norwich Corporation granted the lease of a portion of the Old City Gaol for a term of ninety-nine years in order to house a library. The annual rent was £1.

The beginning of the nineteenth century was also the time of naval triumph for Norfolk's most eminent son, Vice Admiral Lord Horatio Nelson. He had gained his love of the sea growing up on the coast in Brancaster and later attended Norwich School for a period. The press was always ready to report his every move. On 14 April 1801 it was able to report the destruction of the Danish fleet in Copenhagen Bay by the British fleet under the immediate command of Lord Nelson. It said that the news was conveyed to Norwich by coach, which entered the city with colours flying; the Volunteer corps paraded in the Market Place and fired a feu de joie, and the bells of St Peter Mancroft and of other churches were rung.

The Adam and Eve in Norwich is claimed to be the oldest pub in the city, with earliest references from 1249

Great Yarmouth Quayside, by J.W. Whymper, nineteenth century

It was on 21 October 1805 that Nelson was to gain his greatest victory against the combined French and Spanish fleets at Trafalgar. This was to secure the seas for Great Britain. Ten years later, His Grace the Duke of Wellington (adopted as its own by Norwich where his son was subsequently MP) finally sent Napoleon into exile and British dominance on land as well as sea was complete.

Unsurprisingly, given the new thinking on libraries and education for the working man, the increasing participation of Britain on the world stage and the many inventions of the age such as those highlighted above, the nineteenth century witnessed a dramatic change in the social order of Norfolk. The unprecedented new job opportunities in firms that would become household names, such as the Norwich Union (founded 1797 by Thomas Bignold; now named Aviva), Colmans (established 1814) and Boulton and Paul

Surrey House, headquarters to Aviva (formally Norwich Union) was designed by George Skipper between 1900 and 1910 and is a classic example of Edwardian architecture

(started as an ironmongers' shop in 1797 in Norwich) and, increasingly, shoe manufacturers – two of which owned the famous brands of Start-rite and Van Dal, meant that by working hard and upward social mobility was no longer an impossible dream. As remarked above, the railway came to Norfolk from 1844 which, among other things, facilitated the boom in Norfolk coastal towns as people could now easily take a day out. The leisured classes also came to build fine mansions and experience the bracing sea air.

While true that the standard of rural housing remained largely appalling, and drunkenness was rife in some areas (Norwich alone had seven large breweries and many 'unofficial' ones), as the end of Queen Victoria's reign approached in 1901 there were many bright spots in daily life with the county's capital undoubtedly seen as a city 'on the up' in many ways.

Edwardian Norwich 1901–10 and the years leading up to war

> Never yet did a stranger visit Norwich and wander with an intelligent eye through its sinuous streets without experiencing that indescribable charm and delight consequent upon the succession of picturesque prospects which burst upon the view in the numerous combinations of medieval ecclesiastical architecture with the bustle and stir of mercantile establishments.
> *Citizens of No Mean City*, Jarrold, London and Norwich, April 1910

By the turn of the twentieth century, Norwich had become an Edwardian industrial powerhouse with some of the firms destined to play a vital role in the upcoming war. These included Boulton and Paul, already producing virtually anything in metal from wire netting to aircraft bodies; Colman's, who cut down on the acreage given over to mustard production for the duration of hostilities in order to grow more essential crops and were to see 921 men join up, including four of the seven directors; Howlett and White, and many other shoe manufacturers, who together made literally millions of pairs of what was universally agreed to be the perfect marching boot for the British and Allied armies; and Caley's who produced chocolate bars which were sent to hundreds of thousands of troops on the front lines. 'Caley's Marching Chocolate' was especially popular and can still be bought in Norwich.

A plaque close to St Andrew's Hall showing the Norwich coat of arms and Latin text: MDCCCCII Floreat Norvicvm, which translates as '1902 May Norwich Flourish'. The design of this coat of arms is based on a fifteenth-century seal, and features Norwich Castle and the Royal Lion of England

Norwich had also been famous since Victorian times for beer production with at least seven large breweries, such as Youngs, Crawshay and Youngs, and Bullards, along with dozens of malthouses. This was very much a mixed blessing as it is estimated that the city had over 500 public houses, many of which were unlicensed, being nothing more than the front rooms of wretched houses in areas of the city such as Coslany where poverty was rife. City magistrates continually ordered that such establishments, which found it easy to buy a barrel of ale from a brewery literally 'up the road' and sell it in an attempt to eke out a living, be closed down only for another to open up, often next door or nearby.

It was felt morally necessary to offer help against the demon drink, which was a significant problem and was one factor in the often poor physical condition of those offering themselves for recruitment to the army. The Independent Order of Rechabites, Temperance Friendly Society, announced that it 'admits Males and Females, Adults and Juveniles, to Membership', and had the slogan: 'We Live in Deeds Not Words'. The United Kingdom Provident Institution claimed to be 'The Best Office for Abstainers'. Drunkenness was a continual theme in the local courts of Norwich.

The city was also a main Empire centre for the banking and insurance industries. The famous Norwich Union Insurance Company had its exquisite headquarters in Surrey Street, built by George Skipper from imported Italian marble in 1903/4 (it is magnificent and still fully open to view by the public today). Total funds in 1908 amounted to £8,823,303. Gurney's Bank, now part of Barclays, created the phrase, common at the time, 'as rich as the Gurneys'. Farrows Bank Ltd operated from the Market Place; advertisements in the local press read: 'It Caters for All Classes, It Offers Sound Security'.

Shopping was very much up-to-the-minute. Norwich boasted one of the finest arcades of shops outside of London – The Royal Arcade, designed by George Skipper, which looks almost exactly the same as it did in the early 1900s. There were some fine stores, too. One, still very much thriving today, was Jarrold. In Edwardian times it advertised itself in various ways, including as 'a travelling goods specialist', 'The Noted Bookshop' and 'The Noted Gift House', all of which it still is; but before the Great War it also boasted 'Jarrold's Select Library – Free Use to an Entire Family of a well-appointed Reading Room; subscriptions from 10/6 per Annum'. Other stores included Tuxford Trunks, which asked: 'Are your trunks all right? Tuxford Trunks are Porter-proof. No 3 Back-of-the-Inns, Norwich'. Messrs Arthur Bunting and Co Ltd of St Stephen's Corner and Rampant Horse Street described itself as being 'Quite in the front rank of the leading Drapery and Furnishing Houses of Norwich.'

Many were quick to adapt to change. As flying became the latest very exciting, often fatal in these early days, activity for the daring, the *Eastern*

Daily Press reported that confectioners, Snelling's, of Rampant Horse Street, had a new delicacy on offer: aviation cakes. 'Very light and easily digestible', they were on sale for one shilling in a choice of nine flavours: almond, cherry, walnut, rose, orange, lemon, violet, chocolate and coffee.

Plain false teeth could be obtained from a dentist in Castle Mall for one guinea and those made from gold and Vulcanite were offered for three times that figure. Hair pomade and all sorts of medicines, some of which made highly dubious claims such as warding off consumption, were easily available. H.A. King of 38 Exchange Street was advertising that it could provide 'Artificial Eyes Carefully Fitted'. Another advertisement for hair lotion advised: 'Don't lose your hair! Keep your employment! Flowing locks and luscious lashes guaranteed with Johnson's Hair Pomade!' Those lacking energy were advised to purchase 'Pratt's Pink Pills for Pale People'.

The *Norfolk Chronicle and Norwich Gazette* was much devoted to ladies' fashion and it carried the following advertisement:

TO THE LADIES OF EAST ANGLIA. Many Corset Manufacturers (particularly those with no designers of their own) were caught unawares by this year's great change of fashion and now see that THEY MISREAD THE SIGNAL FROM PARIS with the result that they now find themselves loaded with heavy stocks of unsaleable corsets. This sort of thing cannot be too strongly deprecated; and to offset it we have devoted the sum of £17,854 for REDUCING the prices of ten of the favourite models of Royal Worcester Kidfitting Corsets...all of which hold the SILVER SEAL CERTIFICATE of the London Institute of Hygiene. Agents in Yarmouth, Lowestoft, King's Lynn, Norwich etc.

This era also saw the emergence of the motor car, and Mann Egerton of Norwich had the following available as advertised in *The Eastern Daily Press* of 1916, two years into the conflict – some of them are pre-war models:

12hp 1913 Talbot Coupe, £400; 25hp 1909 De Dion Coupe, £190; 10hp 1912 Austin, £200; 6hp 1907 Rover, £30; 28hp Lanchester, £275; 15.9hp Arrol-Johnston, £160; 25hp 1912 Daimler limousine, £550; 20hp Rolls Royce Landaulette, £250; and 28hp Delauney Belleville Shooting Brake, £100.

Bicycles were also popular and the paper was advertising 'The Raleigh All Steel Bicycle', intriguingly 'guaranteed forever (agents all over Norfolk)'. It could be delivered to your door for £3 19s 9d. The paper also featured a campaign to repair the Dereham Road, which it considered unsafe for cyclists.

Agricultural work was the most common way of earning a living in Norfolk and wages for agricultural workers during this period were about £75 a year. There was also a great call for servants. *The Eastern Daily Press* daily carried advertisements for Cook-Housekeepers at wages of £75, £65, or £45 a year, dependent on experience. Another agency, advertising in the *Diss Express* called for Nurses, Housemaids, Parlour maids, Cooks, Second Housemaids, Under Housemaids, Cooks-General, Kitchen maids, Scullery Maids, and Between Maids at yearly salaries £10 to £30. Applicants were to call in person at 78, Prince of Wales Road (now an estate agent). When people went shopping, milk cost 2d a pint, a pound of bacon was a shilling and a loaf of bread just over 5d (there were twelve pennies (d) to a shilling and twenty shillings to a pound.

Norwich engineers were the proud builders of a fine citywide tram network, operational from 1901, although during the first years of the Great War, lighting the cars at night while not showing a light to the enemy was to prove problematic. Another achievement which was to cause even greater difficulty with regard to making the city invisible to passing Zeppelins was the project, headed by city electrical engineer, F.M. Long, which installed 1,750 electric lights in the streets between 1911 and 1913.

Norwich has always managed to produce people of invention and vision in all manner of fields from banking and insurance to mustard, chocolate, anaesthetics and ballooning. One whose ideas did not materialise, but which might have had a dramatic impact on the war, was a Mr W.J. Botterill who, in 1909, proposed a new plan for Norfolk to be the premier naval base for Great Britain (which at the time was Rosyth in Scotland). He proposed a canal from the River Yare at Berney Arms to Norwich, with a massive naval base four miles outside Norwich at Rockland Broad. Finally, he suggested a 240 mile ship canal across England from the North Sea to the Bristol Channel. Quite a few major cities would thus become docks with links to the sea, including Cambridge, Bedford and Oxford. Money permitting, a further channel could be dug linking Oxford and Birmingham. Alas, this never came to be as the expense would have been too great and this was at a time when many were pointing out the antiquity of some ships in the navy and the need for replacement.

The crime and punishment sections of local newspapers and magazines in the Edwardian period contain a varied mix of cases as in any large city. They are not always without humour – here are two from the *Eastern Daily Press*.

The first was heard at Norfolk Quarter sessions and concerned fowl-stealing charges:

> John Henry Crittoph, Baker, pleaded not guilty to stealing 25 game fowls, property of Ernest Edward Fish of Scottow. The prosecutor said he missed the fowls on Feb eighth from their portable fowl houses. The leather hinge of one of the doors had been cut through. Mr Dodson said to the witness 'Anyhow they were not in the habit of tearing the hinges off the doors of their huts' (laughter). Witness 'No'. Robert Lee said he saw the 25 fowls in a cart covered with a net. The prisoner said he had bought the fowls from a man in Ber Street, Norwich. The Jury returned the verdict that the prisoner was not guilty of stealing the fowls, but of receiving them knowing them to have been stolen. The prisoner was sentenced to six weeks with hard labour.

The second concerned a motor car:

> Frederick Charles Barber, chauffeur, was summoned for driving a motor at a speed dangerous to the public in Church Street. From the evidence of Inspector William Pile, it appeared that seeing the defendant driving fast, he called for him to stop. He put the pace at about twenty miles an hour. There were pedestrians about at the time. The defendant said that his car was six years old and noisy. He put his speed at about ten miles an hour. The Chairman said that the magistrates were unanimously of the opinion that the case was proved. Defendant would be fined 10s with 10s costs.

In the nation as a whole, the Edwardian period – roughly from 1901 to the outbreak of war – is often seen as a 'golden' time; of regattas on the Thames, of horse-racing, of rich and opulent fashions, and politically, of great world power. One man who exemplified this was the new king, Edward VII. Following the restraint of the old queen's declining years, the nation wanted a party and the king was more than happy to lead it. In reality, England's dominance was already starting to decline and many historians trace the break-up of the British Empire directly to this period. Sometimes it is written that England as a whole was 'partying to conflict'. Both America and Germany were overtaking England in the efficiency of manufacturing processes, and with the sinking of three British cruisers – the *Hogue*, *Aboukir* and *Cressy* – in 1915 within the space of ninety minutes by one German U-boat, a shocked public realised that British naval dominance was by no means a given any longer.

Norwich itself was changing, too. The importance of the city was recognised when, on 25 October 1909, King Edward VII became the first monarch to visit Norwich since Charles II, 238 years previously. From 1910 the mayor became a lord mayor – one of only fifteen cities in the kingdom to be granted this distinction. George V was to visit the city on 28 June 1911, a mere six days after his coronation. Norwich undoubtedly had growing clout.

Politically, this was a transformative time for women's rights. From 1907 women could stand for the city council, the first elected being Mabel Clarkson in 1913. Emmeline Pankhurst spoke above male cat-calls at St Andrew's Hall in December 1912 (apparently the main chant to drown her out was 'On the Ball, City' which could be heard all over the city each time 'the Canaries' played at home). Just after the war, Norwich became the first city in the country to have a female lord mayor, Ethel Colman, daughter of Jeremiah James Colman – her sister, Helen, acted as lady mayoress.

As well as owning Norwich's premier department store and private library, the Jarrold family also operated a printing works and in 1910 they published *Citizens of No Mean City* which had this to say:

Few cities are more beautifully situated than Norwich, through which winds the meandering Wensum, while the waterways on every hand, penetrating or bounding its pleasant suburbs, almost enclose as in a silvery cincture, the capital of the county of the Broads.

John Jarrold Printing Museum

Looking at artwork and old photographs of the period it does, indeed, appear beautiful in a more rural sense than we know it today and in one aspect in particular, this was to have a direct bearing on the feeding of the troops. In Tudor times, Norwich had been described as 'a city in an orchard or an orchard in a city', so great were the number and varieties of apple trees to be seen. In the first part of the century the apple crop was still of great importance and apples – often with plums – were a staple of soldiers on the front line. So plentiful were the supplies that rations containing apples were the butt of many military jokes and great was the joy and hilarity when an apple-less meal was produced. It is practically impossible to see an apple tree in central Norwich today and many varieties have been lost. We can only wonder at the magic of some of the names – Norwich Jubilee; Caroline, from Blickling (named after Lord Suffield's wife); Norfolk Nonpareil; Royal Coast Russet; St Magdalen; and Colonel Harbord's Pippin.

Norwich was in the news for an altogether different reason in 1912 – flooding caused by excessive rain. On 27 August the city's lights went out as the electric power station failed, under 6 ft of water. Over 3,500 houses were affected, many in the poverty-stricken Yards, running down to the river in the north of the city. These were the people (referred to earlier) who tried everything to make ends meet, including selling beer from their front room. They had no voice and had been largely ignored for a long time, except when they appeared in court, which was every week, most often for drunkenness, immoral behaviour, swearing and stealing. Now the national press took up their case, not entirely out of the goodness of their hearts as there was a growing fear that war may be coming and people from these backgrounds would be needed in the armed forces. On the positive side there

A flood level plaque was hung on the walls beside the River Wensum after the great flooding of 1912

were many tales of friendship and heroism as people sailed up the streets in whatever boats they could find, distributing food and warm drinks. Local shops and manufacturers such as Caley's provided drinks of chocolate and milk in bottles with a loop of string on the neck, which were passed to upper windows on a pole with a hook on the end.

Thus all was not well at this time – certainly Norwich was not enjoying a magical 'Edwardian summer' any more than the rest of the country. However, if you had a job and a decent home, life could seem rosy. Even if you did not, there was a feeling that life could change, education and, increasingly, votes, were for everyone, and there were many wonders to engage the mind. The overall feeling was a positive one of pride, both in the country and the city, exemplified by a contemporary local writer, Herbert Leeds. He is talking of life just before the war:

A great wave of industrial prosperity was passing over the country, and Norfolk, especially its capital, was more or less directly feeling its stimulus. Employment was brisk, money was circulating freely, an air of general well-being existed.

Peace Souvenir, Norwich War Record, Jarrold and Sons Ltd, 1919.

'Cloudesley Walks to Work'

A fictional story set in the early nineteenth century and based on genuine news reports in the local papers of the day.

The year is 1814 and a young clerk to the insurance firm of The Norwich County and Municipal Insurance Company, which has offices overlooking the Market Place, is making his way to work. His first name is Cloudesley, which is quite a popular name of the time. The job he has as clerk is a pretty good one, although not fabulously well paid to begin with but, yes, he is on his way.

Cloudesley has to tread carefully as he crosses the Marketplace to avoid the blood and offal discarded by the butchers who are just setting up shop. There are also leather merchants, coffee dealers, beer sellers, vendors of hot potatoes, bread makers and bakers of the famous Norwich Biscuit, which is filling but probably 50 per cent chalk; he needs to watch that he is not hit by the waste they throw from their stalls without looking! Everything is just left to drain away down to the bottom of the square where a pack of dogs laps up the disgusting-looking mess.

There is a wretched man in a pen – he is shirtless and has a scarred back; several people are laughing, throwing rotten vegetables at him. He has obviously been there all night, having been flogged for drunkenness or maybe lewd behaviour. Being a kind sort of chap, Cloudesley passes his flask of weak beer through the bars to the man – cold water is far too dangerous to drink – and the pitiful prisoner grasps it thankfully, downing it in one.

It's only ever men who you see being punished in the Market Place – most days there is at least one flogging and several left in cages like the chap this morning. This does not mean that women don't swear, fight, steal or get drunk – the courts are full of them as a matter of fact. No, it's just that their punishment is always courtesy of the ducking stool at Fye Bridge, near Tombland.

*Norwich Market in 1806 by John Sell Cotman: this is how Cloudesley would have
seen it on a busy day*

The main thing, though, is the smell, and it is something our hero can
never get over. He cannot understand why people let themselves smell so
rank – Cloudesley insists on going to the public bathhouse once every few
weeks, whether he feels dirty or not. He passes a group of well-dressed
people, each of whom has an orange, pricked all over, in front of their nose
to ward off the worst of it. Oranges are very expensive; one day, maybe, he
will treat himself.

On the whole, the Market Place has happy memories for him. It is here
that nine years before he had witnessed the wonderful news of Admiral Lord
Nelson's victory over the combined French and Spanish fleets at Trafalgar.
The news was conveyed to the city by coach which arrived colours flying
to the cheers of the crowd. The Volunteer Corps paraded and the bells of St
Peter Mancroft were rung throughout the day, although the news was cast
in shadow by the death of the hero of the Nile and Trafalgar. A giant ox was
roasted in the pub on the corner.

Truth be told, Cloudesley is just a little tired this morning. Last night he and a group of the clerks had gone to Mrs Peck's Coffee and Ale House on Gentleman's Walk. The poster had read:

To be seen alive in a genteel room at Mrs Peck's Coffee and Ale House, Market Place, Norwich, the largest Rattlesnake ever seen in England, 42 years old, near nine ft long, in full health and vigour. He is well secured so that Ladies and Gentlemen may view him without the least danger. He has not taken any sustenance for 11 months. Admittance, Ladies and Gentlemen 1s; working people and children 6d.

It was a bit of a mystery why this particular creature was not eating – Norwich had many such 'exhibits' and the usual thing was that people would be admitted at half price if they brought something – a live mouse or a rat, say – to feed to the animal.

Afterwards, being in fine spirits, the party could not resist going just up the road to the White Hart, Rampant Horse Street, to see the famous 'counting pig'. It might have been the beer, but it was amazing – customers were invited to hold up a number of fingers and lo! The fat old porker would scrape a paw on the ground the right number of times! Cloudesley couldn't help thinking that maybe, somewhere out of sight, was a man with a pointed stick, poking the poor thing…

So what's going on in 'No Mean City' as the people so proudly called it? How are things?

There is great nervousness about a probable French invasion, which could well happen via Weybourne. The greatest ever British General, Wellington, may have blunted Napoleon's glories and sent him into exile, but there were almost weekly rumours of his escape. Besides, the French absolutely detested us, a feeling returned with vigour. The largest pub on Gentleman's Walk, owned by Alderman Davey – he who has recently invented an iron coffin, said to be completely safe against body snatchers – has an effigy of the strutting Corsican being skewered on a giant fork by John Bull. The pub is very popular.

From the coast to the top of Norwich Castle are a series of wooden beacons ready to be fired if the French are spotted. Thus Norwich would know within minutes if the dreaded enemy has landed.

Cloudesley always arrives early for work as he likes to take a look at the newspaper before the five fellow clerks with whom he shares an office arrive. He sits at his tall wooden stool and spreads the *Norfolk Chronicle and Norwich Gazette* out on his desk.

Several items catch his eye. The population of Norfolk is returned as 274,221, of whom 130,249 were males and 143,972 females. However, as about 4,000 men are away in Wellington's army, the sexes are slightly more equal than that figure suggests.

Coudesley also reads that 247,000 quarts of soup are weekly being given to the poor. However, all is not doom and gloom as the Palace Workhouse – down by the old Palace of the Duke of Norfolk, the one who lost his head planning to marry Mary, Queen of Scots – reports that numbers of inmates has fallen from 1,027 to 425.

Wheat has risen from 146 shillings per quarter at the beginning of the month to 180 at the end. Various ruses are being tried to get people to eat less bread. 'The officers of the West Norfolk Militia', the paper states, 'have entirely left off the use of bread at their mess, and have forbid the use of puddings and pies, except the crust is made of rice or potatoes, which they eat in a variety of shapes as a substitute for bread. Nurses are advised to use linseed meal and water instead of bread and milk in making poultices.'

He is pleased to read that repairs to the disastrous fire in the roof of Norwich Cathedral, caused by careless workmen and estimated to be costing over £500, are almost complete.

Oh lucky man! The winner of the Irish lottery, Mr Charles Weston, is a banker living in Norwich and is today richer to the tune of £15,000.

Chapelfield, where he often eats his lunch, is berated by a leading architect as being 'a very cockneyfied and badly laid out public space'.

The man previously cleared by Magistrates for knocking down and stealing the wallet from an old soldier in Castle Ditches – who subsequently died – has had an attack of conscience and confessed, even though he knows he will be hanged.

Under a section called 'Curious Notes' he reads of a businessman, Ainsworth Crisp, who has a shop in London Street and lives upstairs. He has had a coffin made of solid English oak, with a silver plaque on the outside giving his name; only the exact date needs to be filled in. This coffin is kept in the corner of his bedroom and is used as a cupboard.

A lady in the letters column complains that Cromer is become far too expensive as regards lodging in the season, but is pleased that this will keep out the troublesome London Cockney. As regards Happisburgh, one reader agrees with Walter Rye who, in a famous account of 1885, scathingly said that no book was to be found there; everyone is in bed by nine; dullness reigns supreme; and William Cowper, the poet, went there, but went mad and he does not wonder at it.

Much of the paper is filled with crime, which is rampant, there being no law enforcement officers employed by the authorities. It is true that Aldermen can appoint men with temporary powers to arrest and detain troublemakers but, being usually the chief troublemakers themselves, they were notoriously subject to bribes and worse.

Four men have been hanged in Norwich – two for robbing the Rectory at North Walsham; one for stealing a cow and three heifers, and one for stealing six sheep. The hangings took place at the entrance to the castle in front of enthusiastic crowds. Food and drink was sold and there was much singing and general merriment until the arrival of the prisoners when 'an awful silence fell'. The paper reports that one man, a well-known criminal, 34 years old and dressed in fine clothes, attracted considerable attention from several well-dressed ladies.

At Norwich Quarter Sessions John William Smith was charged with stealing a silver spoon from the Waggon and Horses public-house, the property of William Smith, and a coat, the property of Michael Callow, from the Crown Inn, St Stephens. He was sentenced to seven years' transportation.

Politically, Cloudesley is neither committed to the Whigs nor the Tories. Sometimes, he goes along to the *Norwich Revolution Society* which meets at the Blue Bell and which, despite its alarming name seems more of a heavy drinking club than anything else. The alternative is the *Norwich Patriotic Society*, but that appears much the same. No, his future probably lay not in politics, but in insurance – he greatly admires Mr Thomas Bignold who started something called *The Norwich Union Insurance Company* a mere twenty years ago, at the age of 36, as he was unable to insure himself against highwaymen (who are a curse whenever a respectable person ventures outside the city walls). Norwich Union is fast becoming a great English commercial company.

Thomas Bignold is very much a hero of young people hereabouts and Cloudesley chuckles to himself as he reads of his latest exploit. The *Chronicle* relates that, not one to suffer fools gladly, he has refused insurance to a man he disliked who wanted cover against being bitten by a mad dog on the grounds that should a dog do this, it would assuredly be sane. There is much idle talk of his son, Samuel, taking over the company as his father is becoming increasingly erratic, but Cloudesley thinks the press would not like this as it would certainly have less to write about.

He is much taken with the report about a library which may open in the Guildhall building – the cost of membership as proposed is high, no doubt to detract ruffians, but the idea of being able to borrow books is pretty exciting; he reads a letter in the *Chronicle* from a Parson who thinks that allowing the working man to gain knowledge will inevitably lead to them becoming discontented with their lot and end in disaster. Hmm … it's a thought.

Life expectancy in 1814 is about 40 years. Cloudesley will do better than this because he is temperate in his habits, takes a good wash every now and again and has a respectable career which will mean a reasonable house. He hopes to meet a local girl to settle down with and bearing this in mind will no doubt find himself at six this evening parading up and down Gentleman's Walk, which is exactly what it says it is, and may fall into a coffee shop now and again to rest and set the world to rights – especially regarding that troublesome French so-called 'Emperor' – with his fellows. Life is good! He picks up an invoice from the pile in front of him, nods 'Hi' to Tim, a fellow clerk who is just coming in the door, and begins his day's labours.

Lost Villages

There are estimated to be over 200 lost villages in Norfolk, many of them medieval. *East Anglian Archaeology* has some excellent material on the subject. Here is a list of just a few: Anmer; Babingley, where St Felix may have landed in about AD 630; Barton Bendish – some earthworks remain; Beachamwell – see text for news of a find made there; Bixley, with the only church in England dedicated to St Wandregesilius; Clare, north of Cromer, lost to erosion; Egmere; Felbrigg; Heckingham, located on several different sites until medieval period; Jerpestun, near Loddon; Shipden, legendary village off Cromer lost to the sea gradually beginning with part of the graveyard in 1336 (often called the 'Atlantis of Norfolk': more details Chapter 2); West Tofts, now part of the Stanford Training Area; and Wighton, where Iron Age and Roman settlement sites have been found.

Notes

1. Quoted in: Rev. D.J. Stewart 'Notes on Norwich Cathedral', Norfolk and Norwich Archaeological Journal, 1875.
2. A most interesting discussion of Bishop de Losinga's origins, education, character and talents, including his literary skills, can be found in *Memoir of William Herbert de Losinga, First Bishop of Norwich* by the Rev W.T. Spurdens published by Norfolk and Norwich Archaeological Society in their journal of 1852. In addition, a subject of spirited debate in the nineteenth century was whether he, as well as many of the clergy after the Conquest, was married. It is claimed that his three predecessors at Thetford had been. The Rev. Augustus Jessop DD presents his evidence in a lively article 'On Married Clergy in Norfolk in the Thirteenth Century' in *Norfolk archaeology, or, Miscellaneous tracts relating to the antiquities of the county of Norfolk*, pp.187–200, published 1884.
3. *Foxe's Book of Martyrs*, John Foxe, 1516–1587; several editions are available for study in the British Library, London.
4. The church of Wiggenhall St Mary is reputed to have a Victorian organ that plays itself – see Chapter 3.
5. *Introduction to Norfolk and Norwich Archaeological Society: or Miscellaneous tracts relating to the antiquities of the county of Norfolk* Vol 1, Norwich, Charles Muskett, Old Haymarket 1847.
6. More details of Charles Dickens and the use of Norfolk in his novels: *The World of Charles Dickens* by Stephen Browning (Halsgrove).
7. Notions of a good diet vary throughout the centuries. As discussed in Chapter 4, modern man could not have endured Stone Age food, nor, most probably, that of medieval and Tudor times. An example of the breakfast of the 5th Earl of Northumberland and his lady is given in their *Household Book,* which was begun in 1512: 'Furst, a loof of Brede in Trenchors' [slices], Manchetts [rolls], a quart of beer, a quart of wine, half a chyne of mutton or els a chine of beif boiled.' The vast array of

staff were allocated their own very precise breakfasts dependent on status. A Gentleman Usher, for example, could have 'A loofe of Brede a Pottel of Bere and a Pece of Saltfische' while a Household Clerk was allowed an extra portion of fish: 'A loofe of Brede, a Pottel of Bere and two Peces of Saltfische'.

8. In All Saints' Church, Upper Sheringham is a monument which reads 'Here Lyeth the Body of Thomas Heath, son of Mr William Heath, of Norwich, wood chapman, who was robbed and murdered the 4 day of February, 1633.'

9. There is a memorial stone in St Nicholas Chapel to a 'Robinson Crusoe', who died on 6 August 1704. The famous novel was published in 1719 and, although there is no proof, it seems highly plausible that Defoe could have seen the name in the chapel and used it, slightly modified.

10. See the *Witches of Salem* and notes on St Anthony's Fire.

11. Lord Bulwer-Lytton led a busy life as a politician (Secretary of State for the Colonies 1858–9), almost a king (he was offered the crown of Greece in 1862 but declined) and as a prolific novelist, once supremely popular, although his literary reputation has not stood the test of time. He is credited with the expressions 'the pen is mightier than the sword', and 'the great unwashed'. His opening line to the novel *Paul Clifford* (1830) – 'It was a dark and stormy night' – has inspired a competition run by the San Jose State University to find the worst possible beginning to a novel and which currently attracts over 10,000 entries each year. For details of the competition, the six extremely funny books that have resulted, and how to enter, check out www.bulwer-lytton.com.

12. The writer attended King Edward VII Grammar School for his secondary education.

13. *Norfolk and Norwich Archaeological Society Journal* 1847.

14. Peter Heylyn, an exact contemporary of Norwich's celebrated writer, Sir Thomas Browne, was the author of many historical works and paints a vivid portrait of his age. He graduated from Magdalen College, Oxford at the age of 16 and became a leading supporter of King Charles II, leading to loss of his preferments under the Commonwealth. These were restored later by the crown, but by this time his health was deteriorating. Apart from the above, his most ambitious book was a history of the whole world

described as: ' Cosmography in four books, containing the choreography and history of the whole world and all the principal kingdoms, provinces, seas, and the isles thereof, with an accurate and approved index of all the kingdoms, provinces, countries, inhabitants, people, cities, mountains, rivers, seas, islands, forts, bays, capes, forests etc of any remarque in the whole world.' It contains the first known account of Australia. This is available to study in the British Library.

15. Francis Blomefield (1705–52) wrote a renowned account of Norfolk. A new and complete edition, in ten volumes royal octavo, of *Blomefield's Topographical history of the county of Norfolk*, etc. (W. Miller London, 1804). Now in the British Library.

16. Full article: *Norfolk archaeology, or, Miscellaneous tracts relating to the antiquities of the county of Norfolk, Norfolk and Norwich Archaeological Society Journal* 1888, pp 271-6.

17. Mr A.C. Savin was a noted expert on fossils.

18. Taken from *Norfolk Coast in the Great War,* Stephen Browning (Pen and Sword 2017).

19. Compare this with the valuations in 1334 of Norwich and Great Yarmouth given later in the chapter.

20. A wonderfully detailed account of his 'wake' at the monastery exists. It shows that a man was employed for three days prior to slaughter cattle and the surrounding countryside was swept of chickens, geese and capons. Bought in were thirteen barrels of beer, twenty-seven barrels of ale, fifteen gallons of wine, 1,300 eggs, twenty gallons of milk, eight of cream, forty-one pigs and forty-nine calves. A barber was employed for five days to smarten up the monks.

21. The Paston Letters form one of the great collections of English letters, giving an incomparable account of life in fifteenth-century England, and Norfolk in particular. The British Library houses over 100 books and articles based on the letters. A recommended book with an overview of the letters in modern English is given in the Bibliography.

22. See also remarks on St Anthony's Fire, Chapter 3 Central Norfolk – east.

23. *Norfolk archaeology, or, Miscellaneous tracts relating to the antiquities of the county of Norfolk, Norfolk and Norwich Archaeological Society,* Henry Harrod, Hon. Sec.,1852.

24. Duleep Singh surrendered his lands in the Punjab, and the Koh-i-Noor Diamond – 105.6 carats and now part of the Queen Mother's Crown – to the British at the age of 10 in 1849. Coming to England, he was befriended by Queen Victoria and settled in Elveden Hall. In later life, he fought to regain his lands but to no avail. Prince Frederick was his second son.

25. Being flogged, bullied and worse was seen as a rite of passage for many schoolboys in the eighteenth and nineteenth centuries. Cowper's near contemporary, novelist Anthony Trollope (1815–1882), wrote about one of his tormentors: 'He must have known me had he seen me as he was wont to see me, for he was in the habit of flogging me constantly. Perhaps he did not recognise me by my face'. The so-called 'Great Rebellion' at Winchester in 1793 was aimed at curtailing 'spying' by the Head and the senior boys at Harrow went on strike in 1808 against the proposed restriction of flogging rights. (*When Schooldays Were Fun*, Stephen Browning, Halsgrove, 2010).

26. G.E. Fox, Esq., F.S.A. (1889) 'Roman Norfolk'. *Archaeological Journal 46*. http://archaeologydataservice.ac.uk/

27. Robert Fitch Esq, F.S.A., F.G.S. Etc *Journal of the Norfolk and Norwich Archaeological Society*, Vol 6.

28. See *Our Mutual Friend*, published 1864-5, and in particular, Silas Wegg, who goes to great lengths to buy back his amputated leg.

Bibliography

AA Media Ltd (2014) *AA Guide to Norfolk and Suffolk*

An Historical Atlas of Norfolk, 3rd edition, Chichester, Phillimore

Ashwin, T. and Davison, A. (ed.) *Late Neolithic and Bronze Age Norfolk*

Bance Peter. (2009) *Sovereign, Squire and Rebel Maharajah Duleep Singh*, Coronet House Publishing

Bilney, Thomas. (1831) *A Brief Account of Thomas Bilney; to which are subjoined his letters to Bishop Tonstal*, available for study at the British Library, Kings Cross, London

Blomefield, Francis, (1804) A *new and complete edition, in ten volumes royal octavo, of Blomefield's Topographical history of the county of Norfolk, etc.* W. Miller London, available for study at the British Library

Browning, Stephen, (2009) *Discover Norwich*, Halsgrove

Browning, Stephen, (2010) *When Schooldays Were Fun*, Halsgrove

Browning, Stephen, (2012) *The World of Charles Dickens*, Halsgrove

Browning, Stephen, (2016) *Norwich in the Great War*, Pen and Sword

Browning, Stephen, (2017) *Norfolk Coast in the Great War*, Pen and Sword

Browning, S. and Tink, D. (2013) *The Peddars Way and Norfolk Coast Path*, Halsgrove

Buckley, N. and Buckley, J. (2011) *Norfolk and the Broads,* Horizon Editions

Bulwer-Lytton, Edward. (1832) *Eugene Aram A Tale*, Henry Colburn and Richard Bentley, London

Caley, Rev. W.B. (1898) *A Pictorial and Descriptive Guide to Cromer, Sheringham, The Runtons, Poppyland, William Andrews and Co, London*

Childs, Alan. (1992) Sheringham and Beeston, SB Publications

Cromer and District (1921), Ward Lock and Co

Davis, Norman. (ed.) (2008) *The Paston Letters, A Selection in Modern Spelling*, Oxford University Press

Doyle, Sir Arthur Conan, (1930) *The Penguin Complete Sherlock Holmes*, Penguin

English Heritage (2004) *Heritage Unlocked*

Foxe, John, (1910 edition) Foxe's Book of Martyrs, available for study at the British Library, Kings Cross, London

Hedges, Alfred, (1973) *Great Yarmouth as it Was*, Hendon Publishing Co Ltd

Hepworth, Philip, (1972) *Victorian and Edwardian Norfolk from old photographs*, BT Batsford Ltd, London

Heylyn, P. (1674) *A help to English History, containing a succession of all kings of England etc.....*, T.Basset and T. Wilkinson, London, available for study at the British Library, Kings Cross, London

Hooper, James. (1902) *Jarrold's Illustrated Guide to Cromer*, Jarrold

Jarrold (1910) *Citizens of No Mean City*

Lamont-Brown, R. (1981) *East Anglian Epitaphs*, Acorn Editions

Lawson, A.J., Martin, E.A. and Priddy, D. (1981) *The Barrows of East Anglia*, East Anglian Archaeology

Leeds, Herbert. (ed.) (1919) *Peace Souvenir, Norwich War Record*, Jarrold

Norfolk and Norwich Archaeological Society Journal, various years

Osborne, Mike, (2015) *Defending Norfolk*, Fonthill

Read, Donald, (1972) *Edwardian England*, Harrap

Rye, Walter, (1887) *A Month on the Norfolk Broads on Board the Wherry 'Zoe' and its Tender, the Tub, Lotus*, Simpkin, Marshall and Co

Sympson, C. (1759) *The Genuine Life, Trial and Dying Words of Eugene Aram*, British Library

Tink, D. (2010) *Spirit of Norwich*, PiXZ

Tink, D. and Browning, S. (2010) *Spirit of Norwich Cathedral*, PiXZ

Tink, D. and Browning, S. (2011) *Discover Norfolk, Land of Wide Skies*, Halsgrove

Ward Lock and Co (1920) *Mundesley-On-Sea*

Wilks John (2005) *Walks into History, Norfolk and Suffolk*, Countryside Books

Useful websites

The British Library receives a copy of every book published in the UK, as well as a large proportion of those published overseas and is the largest library by items held (from 150–200 million) in the world. It is most famously situated at 96 Euston Road, London NW1 2DB (Kings Cross tube station) although it has other bases, too. It has some unique material on Norfolk over the centuries. www.bl.uk Tel: 01937 546060

The Norfolk and Norwich Archaeological Society www.nnas.info

The Norfolk Archaeological and Historical Research Group www.nahrg.org.uk

Norfolk Archaeological Trust www.norfarchtrust.org.uk

The Archaeological Journal www.archaeologydataservice.ac.uk

Norfolk Record Office www.archives.norfolk.gov.uk

Libraries – Norfolk County Council www.norfolk.gov.uk/libraries-local-history-and-archives/libraries

Index